MW00636637

Bruised Reeds and Smoldering Wicks

An eight session study on trauma-informed ministry
and working with those who have experienced
adversity or trauma in childhood.

By Rev. Dr. Chris Haughee

The study referencing the original ACE Study is footnoted to draw your attention to the original source material. More information about the ACE Study can be found on the CDC's website: https://www.cdc.gov/violenceprevention/acestudy/

Dedication:

This Bible Study is dedicated to my Lord and Savior, Jesus Christ, and to the children he loves so dearly but are often overlooked and misunderstood. It is also dedicated to my wife, Kimberly, and our two amazing children, Lily and Michael. Thank you for your support and love.

Contents

Introduction to the study

I could tell I had settled into the role of chaplain at the residential treatment facility I work at when the following diagnoses no longer startled me:

- Post-Traumatic Stress Injury;
- Reactive Attachment Disorder of early childhood;
- Attention Deficit/Hyperactivity Disorder;
- Anxiety Disorder;
- Mood Disorder;
- Major Depressive Disorder;
- Neglect of Child; and,
- Sexual Abuse of Child.

Quite a list, to be sure. Behind each of these labels is a child. Not only do these children deserve the best that the Church can manage in terms of care and compassion, these children deserve to be known for something other than their present difficulties or their troubled past.

Children's mental health is an issue not just for Intermountain and other youth group homes that have answered the call to care for the most severe cases of abuse, neglect, or early childhood trauma. The prevalence of adversity in childhood, now firmly established through the Adverse Childhood Experiences Study and subsequent research, should elicit the same response today that was expressed by Intermountain's founder in 1909. Brother William Wesley Van Orsdel, a Methodist minister and circuit rider, answered those who wondered why the church should mobilize to care for vulnerable children: "How could we possibly not do such a thing? Under God, brethren, we cannot continue to let the suffering of children go unchallenged."

> "How could we possibly not do such a thing? Under God, brethren, we cannot continue to let the suffering of children go unchallenged."
> – Brother William Wesley Van Orsdel

That statement launched the ministry that I serve as a chaplain, and that passion for the well-being of children is what fuels the ministry and mission of Intermountain today. The ACE (Adverse Childhood Experience) Study has made clear that not only do children continue to suffer, but that the life-long public health impact of ignoring their need is tremendous. Unfortunately, there is often a disconnection between what hurting children in our communities truly need and the Church's desired effectiveness in mission. I have lived in this disconnected place most of my life, and seek to bridge the gap between the needs of marginalized children and youth and the expressed desire of the Church to meet those needs.

This study serves as a first attempt on my part to frame our knowledge of the brain and human development, trauma's effect of children, and the teachings of the Christian church and its founder, Jesus Christ. It is only a starting point and is by no means exhaustive. As it is an attempt to show the connections between multiple disciplines (science of the brain, human development, theology, education, etc.) it will not delve too deeply into any of these areas. Therefore, the study may appear simplistic in its treatment of these topics for those familiar with the respective fields. For this necessary limitation, I apologize, and would encourage your feedback as further revisions of this study will seek to remedy any glaring deficiencies. I hope that you can bring your expertise to bear in group discussions and fill in your personal experience and knowledge for those omissions that the study undoubtedly will have. That said, I do hope this eight-week study will prompt a much needed discussion on the Church's approaches to trauma, children, and the role ministries might play meeting the challenges children and families face today as they desire healing and wholeness.

A number of edits have gone into this second edition of the curriculum, but my main purpose has stayed the same... the purpose of speaking primarily to childhood trauma. Trauma experienced by children and in our own childhood has a much more significant impact on our physical, spiritual, and emotional well-being as individuals. Indeed, the trauma many experienced as children has an impact that lasts for the rest of an individual's lifetime. In an effort to make this connection more evident, I have included a week near the conclusion of the study specifically focused on adults living in traumatizing situations or with a trauma history. I don't think the issue of a ministry becoming trauma-informed is an either/or proposition when it comes to children's or adult trauma, it's just that my ministry experience has shown me that it is in curbing childhood trauma that the Church has the greatest opportunity to affect lasting societal change.

I am indebted to the over 100 congregations, homeless shelters, small groups and various ministries that engaged with the first edition of the materials. Their feedback and encouragement has hopefully made this second edition better and more comprehensive. I am thankful to you for your willingness to explore these issues within your faith community and for what that might mean for so many that have yet to find a church or fellowship that welcomes them as they work through their trauma story.

Sincerely,

Chaplain Chris Haughee

February 2019

2

Group Leaders: How to use this study

Thank you for agreeing to lead a group through this study! I am hoping that this brief guide will help you make the most of your time with those you are leading.

First, some of the practical aspects of the study. This is what you can expect from each lesson and how you can prepare:

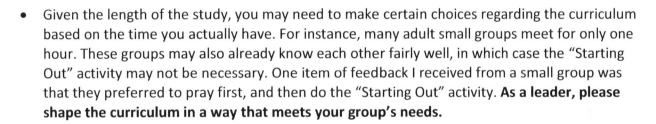

- Each lesson starts with the lesson title, key idea, and key verses. This information is mainly for the group leader, as it is meant to give you a bit of a road map as to where the lesson is going and what the overall objective is.

- **Overall, those that have used the materials report that 60-90 minutes is the time that they found best suited for fully covering the lesson and giving everyone a voice.** This is, of course, dependent on the size of your group and their willingness to open up and discus what can often be very personal and heart-felt issues. I have found that the discussion is best in groups of 4-6 people, so **if you have a larger class, consider breaking up into smaller groups for discussion.**

- Given the length of the study, you may need to make certain choices regarding the curriculum based on the time you actually have. For instance, many adult small groups meet for only one hour. These groups may also already know each other fairly well, in which case the "Starting Out" activity may not be necessary. One item of feedback I received from a small group was that they preferred to pray first, and then do the "Starting Out" activity. **As a leader, please shape the curriculum in a way that meets your group's needs.**

- Bible passages appear in these materials from a variety of translations. If your group is used to bringing their own personal Bibles, you can certainly do readings from your Bibles and not these materials! You may choose to do whatever fits your group best.

- Should anyone in the group reveal a present mental or physical health crisis (either they indicate they are a harm to themselves or others, or are in danger of being harmed by another), does your faith community have a response plan? Having a list of resources in your community ready should a difficult matter come up that is outside the ability of your group to meet is an excellent idea. Also, explaining to your group that confidentiality within the group does not pertain to matters where abuse is observed or suspected, and that this is a matter of mandatory reporting laws put in place to protect vulnerable people.

Other things you may wish to consider include the setting and the expectations for the group. Some small groups have covenants, or listed expectations around confidentiality and protecting the individual member's privacy. Due to the nature of the subjects discussed, you may wish to establish some "ground rules" for your group prior to beginning the study. This will provide a sense of emotional and relational safety for the members of your group.

The felt safety of the space you use is also a consideration for you, the leader. Here is a short list of questions that might be helpful as you are preparing:

- Are you in a room or a space where interruptions will be kept to a minimum and sound won't travel to ears of those outside the group?
- Is it clear to members of the group where a safe place might be to take a break, should the subject matter trigger some difficult feelings within them?
- Is the room comfortable and inviting, setting those who attend at ease instead of making them more anxious?
- If you have a mixed-gender group, might it be helpful to break the group into same-gendered small groups for some of the discussions? Knowing your group, are you going to suggest that individuals keep to the same breakout discussion groups each time, or will you vary the members of each group week-by-week?

The better you can think through these issues prior to your first gathering, the better your chances of having a successful and meaningful group interaction.

A final word about the purpose of the curriculum: it is not meant to be prescriptive, and this will frustrate some within your group. I have tried to add some materials in this edition to address concerns around the **"Well, great… we now know what trauma and adversity does to people, but WHAT DO WE *DO?*"** question. However, even with these additions, I am afraid the study falls short of a "how to" manual for implementing a trauma-informed ministry.

The study is purposefully designed in a way that your group could help define what trauma-informed ministry might look like within your context. If you can help your group understand that their role is to participate in integrating the principles shared in these materials with their wisdom, knowledge, and experience in your community, I think that will help manage expectations and set the group up for success.

Again, thank you for being a leader through these materials. Please reach out via email if you have any additional questions.

Chaplain Chris Haughee

Contact: pastorhaughee@yahoo.com

Week 1: Jesus and the children

Key idea: Jesus welcomes ALL children, even those affected by trauma, toxic stress, or adversity (ACEs).

Key verses:

- "Let the little children come to me…" Luke 18:16
- "A bruised reed he will not break and a smoldering wick he will not snuff out…" Isaiah 42:1-4, referenced in Matthew 12:15-21.

Starting out:

[Each week of the study will start with an introductory question or two, meant to frame the rest of the time together within the greater context of relationship together. Please take the time, each week, to have each person introduce themselves… even if you already know each other… and respond to the questions in turn]

- Go around the circle or table and introduce yourself by sharing the following:
  - your name,
  - your age (or birthday if you prefer!),
  - where you lived as a young child, and
  - a favorite childhood memory

Open the study in prayer:

"Jesus, you are the one Isaiah spoke of when he said that God was sending his special servant: someone who would exhibit the gentleness and compassion of God, so tender that this servant would take little children onto his lap, blessing each and every one. You extend love and care toward those wrestling to make it each day—like a smoldering wick barely burning and a bruised reed struggling to turn to the light of the sun. For those in this room who are feeling or have ever felt that way, we pray. For those in our community that feel this way, we pray. And for our time together in your Word and in discussion together, we pray for your Spirit to enter in. Enlighten our minds and open our hearts, in your precious name. Amen."

From Chaplain Chris to the group:

(please read aloud, with a facilitator reading, or taking turns reading around the circle or table)

A favorite image of mine from childhood is that of the children gathered around Jesus, colorfully illustrated in the Bible I received at my baptism.[1] In the illustration, there is something very tender about the way Jesus cradles the face of the little girl in his hands as well as the nearness of the other

---

[1] Jesus and the Children, copyright 1962, The Standard Publishing Company

children to the Savior. As beautiful as the picture is, the unintended consequence of that picture's imprint on my imagination was a psychological and emotional disconnection between my desire for belonging within the church and my self-identification as someone unworthy of grace. In the picture of Jesus and the children everyone looks so clean: not just physically, but spiritually and emotionally as well.

I can remember thinking, "Certainly, Jesus would have no problem interacting with *these* children— they are so well behaved and attentive!" It seemed a scene a little too fantastic to be real, even as a newly baptized ten year old. I loved the picture not for what it depicted, but for a reality I hope might be true for me some day. I wanted badly to be as clean and well-presented as the children Jesus took time with. I thought, and felt, had I been there I would not have been included. This is the scene as Luke's gospel tells it:

> One day some parents brought their little children to Jesus so he could touch and bless them. But when the disciples saw this, they scolded the parents for bothering him. Then Jesus called for the children and said to the disciples, "Let the children come to me. Don't stop them! For the Kingdom of God belongs to those who are like these children." (Luke 18:15-17, NLT)

The disciples had been with Jesus long enough to know that he lavished attention on those often overlooked. So, why did they scold the parents and push away the children? Could it be that the children coming to Jesus were not like those in the illustration I had in my children's Bible? Perhaps these children were a little disheveled, noisy, messy or poorly behaved?

As I try and envision what would have led the disciples to push the children away from Jesus, I surmise that there must have been some reason to dismiss the children other than their sense that they had nothing to offer Jesus. They had simply seen Jesus include too many outsiders, outcasts, and marginalized people for me to think the children were discouraged from approaching Jesus simply because they were children. No, I think it was because of the *type* of children they were.

As an adult, there is something else about this story I find intriguing. For, in twenty years of working with and speaking to children, I have yet to replicate the artist's scene of Jesus with the children that was depicted in my children's Bible. The children I've worked with? They squirm, pick their nose, lift up skirts and dresses, and do all manner of things to embarrass their parents sitting in the pews. Moreover, they aren't usually as "clean" as these children in the picture appear. The children I know have very "big person"-type problems. They have experienced a great deal of adversity in their few years. Do these children get to come to Jesus?

Does the kingdom of God belong only to the well-behaved, easy-to-manage child, or does it include the child struggling with mental health issues? What does it say of the Church's understanding of God's kingdom if it prefers to work with the well-groomed, well-adjusted, well-behaved child and excludes those that have been hurt by the world and sin and are struggling to overcome it? I would suggest that there is something missing from the Church's understanding of relationships, the Kingdom of God, and Jesus' priorities in ministry, when we either intentionally or unintentionally exclude hurting children from our fellowship.

"Let the little children come to me. Don't stop them!" Jesus said. But what of their hurt, their anger, their aggression, their sadness? *Surely, some other children will do.* Some other children will meet the need of the Church to show its commitment to follow Jesus' command? "The kingdom of God belongs to those who are like these children," Jesus said. If not the hurting children—any of the children I work with each day at Intermountain, and those children hurting and in the shadows of your own community—if not **these** children, than who among us may come?

Discuss:

- In considering the story of Jesus and the little children, why do you think the disciples tried to keep them away?
- What are your impressions of the picture Chaplain Chris refers to from his childhood? What images of Jesus were/are influential in shaping your imagination about him?
- What sort of child would you prefer to have in church and Sunday school? (*Be honest... it's okay!*) How can a church balance its desire for peaceful, safe, worshipful learning environments while allowing for the challenge that some children may present?
- Were there any times, as a child, that you felt excluded from a group? How did it feel? What do you wish would have happened instead?

Read: Matthew 12:9-21

⁹ Going on from that place, he went into their synagogue, ¹⁰ and a man with a shriveled hand was there. Looking for a reason to bring charges against Jesus, they asked him, "Is it lawful to heal on the Sabbath?"

¹¹ He said to them, "If any of you has a sheep and it falls into a pit on the Sabbath, will you not take hold of it and lift it out? ¹² How much more valuable is a person than a sheep! Therefore it is lawful to do good on the Sabbath."

¹³ Then he said to the man, "Stretch out your hand." So he stretched it out and it was completely restored, just as sound as the other. ¹⁴ But the Pharisees went out and plotted how they might kill Jesus.

¹⁵ Aware of this, Jesus withdrew from that place. A large crowd followed him, and he healed all who were ill. ¹⁶ He warned them not to tell others about him. ¹⁷ This was to fulfill what was spoken through the prophet Isaiah:

> ¹⁸ "Here is my servant whom I have chosen,
>   the one I love, in whom I delight;
> I will put my Spirit on him,
>   and he will proclaim justice to the nations.
> ¹⁹ He will not quarrel or cry out;
>   no one will hear his voice in the streets.
> ²⁰ A bruised reed he will not break,
>   and a smoldering wick he will not snuff out,
> till he has brought justice through to victory.
> ²¹   In his name the nations will put their hope." (Isaiah 42:1-4)

Discuss:

- Why do you think Matthew's gospel connects Jesus' right to heal on the Sabbath with the passage from Isaiah?

- Reread verses 19-21. How does the quiet, compassionate ministry approach of Jesus towards "bruised reeds" and "smoldering wicks" provide hope? When have you felt like a bruised reed or smoldering wick?

- What connections do you see between this passage and the one Chaplain Chris referenced earlier? How are the situations of the man with the withered hand and the children brought to Jesus similar?

 Applying science, applying the Word:

Please read aloud the following from Chaplain Chris...

As I begin to share with faith communities why adverse childhood experiences (ACEs) matter and how they can help build more resilient children and healthier communities, I sometimes hear something like this: *'But why does it matter? What difference should it make in ministry?'*

The ACE survey measured the prevalence of ten stress-inducing factors in childhood including abuse, neglect, and substance abuse in the home, and these factors definitely influence those ministries working with these children. The issues children and teens face growing up can be daunting, but the faith-based community can help hurting children by building safe, welcoming communities for all children to thrive.

The 10 factors measured in the original ACE study:
• Emotional Abuse
• Emotional Neglect
• Physical Abuse
• Physical Neglect
• Sexual Abuse
• Substance Abuse
• Domestic Violence
• Mental Illness in the home
• Separation / Divorce
• Incarceration of a family member

My ministry is in Montana—where 17% of children have experienced three or more ACEs, and 1 in 10 have four or more—and my hope is that faith communities could see how their ministries can make a difference. When communities concerned about teen suicide understand that the 10% of children with four or more ACEs have a 1200% greater chance of attempting suicide than their peers, it helps build energy around early childhood interventions.

Learning about ACEs can challenge our prejudices and assumptions about those who struggle with mental health challenges. Trauma and toxic stress in childhood adversely affect our functioning as human beings. Physically, the nervous and endocrine systems of a person with numerous ACEs differs from someone who had a relatively peaceful childhood. Having all those additional stress hormones running through your system wreaks havoc on your health.

Friends, if someone's infirmity doesn't scream out to our sense of sight, touch, or hearing we shouldn't assume it is less significant. *The ACE Study found that the child with six or more ACEs will likely die 20 years earlier than the child with no ACEs.* That is significant.

If the faith communities in Montana want to make a difference in the lives of the 17% of our children with three or more ACEs, we need to think through matters such as these. Likewise, if you want to help children in your community, you will need to learn how ACEs are affecting them!

Parting questions:

- **Have you heard of ACEs before? Did it surprise you that adversity in childhood was so common?**
- **How do you think ACEs are affecting and have affected both children and adults in your church and community?**

Close in Prayer:

"God, we started this study today asking for you to enlighten our minds and open our hearts. You have been in our gathering and you have answered our prayers. There is much for us to consider, much to continue to pray over and about. Help us see how much you love and care for us, even through our own personal traumas and difficulties. Jesus, we ask that your heart of compassion and understanding would be reflected in our lives and in our ministry together. In the name of God our Creator, Christ our Redeemer, and the Spirit who sustains us and intercedes for us. Amen.

Week 2: Advocacy...what is this "trauma-informed" talk all about?

Key idea: In order to advocate for children and families impacted by trauma, your church should consider trauma-informed ministry

Key verses:

- "Speak up for those who cannot speak for themselves, for the rights of all who are destitute. Speak up and judge fairly; defend the rights of the poor and needy." (Proverbs 31:8-9)
- "Praise be to the God and Father of our Lord Jesus Christ, the Father of compassion and the God of all comfort, [4] who comforts us in all our troubles, so that *we can comfort those in any trouble with the comfort we ourselves receive from God.* [5] For just as we share abundantly in the sufferings of Christ, so also our comfort abounds through Christ. [6] If we are distressed, it is for your comfort and salvation; if we are comforted, it is for your comfort, which produces in you patient endurance of the same sufferings we suffer." (2 Cor. 1:3-6)

Starting out:

Go around the circle or table and introduce yourself by sharing the following:

- ○ your name,
- ○ the names and types of any pets you have, and
- ○ a time when someone spoke up for you or defend you. How did it feel?
- ○ [if time] When have you advocated for someone else?

Open the study in prayer:

"God, we praise you that you are indeed the God of all comfort who comes alongside those who suffer and grieve. As you have comforted us, may we bring comfort to others. Jesus, as you have been our advocate, help us to advocate for others. Holy Spirit, you intercede for us even when we cannot put words to our groanings, longing and pain. May we, and our fellowship here, look more and more like this beautiful Trinity of Comforter, Advocate, and Intercessor—all for the sake of a world deeply in need of your love and grace. Amen."

From Chaplain Chris to the group:

(please read aloud, with a facilitator reading, or taking turns reading around the circle or table)

An advocate is someone who speaks on behalf of someone or something that they feel strongly about. Proverbs 31:8-9 says, "Speak up for those who cannot speak for themselves, for the rights of all who are destitute. Speak up and judge fairly; defend the rights of the poor and needy."

Advocacy is a willingness to put some "skin in the game," affecting change in a system, situation, or society through personal effort. It involves speaking out, speaking for, and being there for someone or something outside yourself. It is, ideally, a purely selfless act.

Of course, when we are talking about advocacy in this sense, there is no better example than Jesus. Jesus is God with "skin in the game"—God, who is Spirit (John 4:24; 2 Corinthians 3:17), made flesh (John 1:14) to dwell among us... the incarnation. And, now that Jesus has come and gone, he has left the Spirit with us to empower us to minister to a hurting world as he would if he were still physically present!

Advocacy is also a recognition that, while we can't do everything, we can do something. And, that "something" just might make the world brighter, more beautiful, and more full of hope.

Mother Teresa said, "Not all of us can do great things, but we can all do small things with great love."

As we consider helping children in adversity and those families working through trauma, it's not about having a full-time children's minister or the coolest church nursery in town. In fact—it's not a matter of resources, but relationship. If God causes us to see a need, it's often because God is calling us to do what we can to meet the need.

It's about help, not rescue.

It's about doing what you can and trusting God with the rest.

Speaking of help, who helped you along your way and served as an advocate for you?

By mining your personal history, you are bound to find something you can advocate for, even redeeming something from your past that was difficult or troubling. The great thing is, when you take your past pain and put it into service in the present, you are able to connect with those you are helping in a much more profound and compassionate way. As you have been comforted by God, family and friends, you can comfort others (2 Cor. 1:4).

Communities of faith can be great places for advocacy, and by embracing our role as advocates and ambassadors for the good news of Jesus, we can gain a better sense of purpose as a faith community (2 Cor. 5:20).

Discuss:

- What does it mean to be an advocate? Can you advocate for something or someone if you remain emotionally distant and intellectually removed? Why or why not?
- When have you had an opportunity to "pay it forward" in regards to a kindness done to you or someone advocating on your behalf? What was the situation? How did it make you feel?

- The ACE Study has shown us that adversity affects a significant number of children across social, economic, cultural and racial lines. Who advocates for these children in your community? How can your church be a part of this advocacy?

Read: 2 Corinthians 1:3-6

"Praise be to the God and Father of our Lord Jesus Christ, the Father of compassion and the God of all comfort, [4] who comforts us in all our troubles, so that **we can comfort those in any trouble with the comfort we ourselves receive from God.** [5] For just as we share abundantly in the sufferings of Christ, so also our comfort abounds through Christ. [6] If we are distressed, it is for your comfort and salvation; if we are comforted, it is for your comfort, which produces in you patient endurance of the same sufferings we suffer." (2 Cor. 1:3-6)

Discuss:

- Why do you think Paul refers to God as "the Father of compassion and the God of all comfort?" When have you needed this aspect of God's character in your life?

- According to this passage, why does God comfort us in our troubles? Also, how does this passage make a connection between our sufferings and difficulties and those of Christ?

- Why do you think it makes such a difference when you are going through a difficulty or hardship to know that the person you are being comforted by has also been through the same difficulty? With this in mind, who might be the best "comforters" of children experiencing adversity and trauma?

Applying science, applying the Word:

Please read aloud the following from Chaplain Chris...

There is a growing trend in education, mental health, social services, and health care: *becoming trauma-informed.* For those in ministry, "trauma-informed" can be a confusing phrase, bringing up images we might not naturally associate with the church and its mission and ministry.

Trauma results from something that occurs in a person's life that is experienced as physically or emotionally harmful or life threatening. An event, circumstance or series of events that are traumatic leaves lasting effects on the individual's functioning and mental, physical, social, emotional, or spiritual well-being. It is as much about the person's internal processing of a stressful and difficult situation as it is about the circumstance that results in the trauma. What might traumatize one individual deeply might not as dramatically affect another.

According to the <u>Substance Abuse and Mental Health Services Administration (SAMHSA)</u>, "a program, organization, or system that is **trauma-informed**:

1. *Realizes* the widespread impact of trauma and understands potential paths for recovery;

2. *Recognizes* the signs and symptoms of trauma in clients, families, staff, and others involved with the system;

3. *Responds* by fully integrating knowledge about trauma into policies, procedures, and practices; and

4. Seeks to actively resist *re-traumatization*."

A trauma-informed approach can be implemented in any type of service setting or organization, including churches and para-church ministries, and is distinct from trauma-specific interventions or treatments that are designed specifically to address the consequences of trauma and to facilitate healing, like Intermountain. SAMHSA also prescribes the following six key principles of a trauma-informed approach to service. They are:

1. Safety

2. Trustworthiness and Transparency

3. Peer support

4. Collaboration and mutuality

5. Empowerment, voice and choice

6. Cultural, Historical, and Gender Issues

From SAMHSA's perspective, it is critical to promote the linkage to recovery and resilience for those individuals and families impacted by trauma. This makes sense, doesn't it? It is one thing to recognize when someone in your church or ministry setting has deep woundedness. It is something entirely different to equip yourself and your ministry team to be able to bring healing and hope to that individual or family system.

So, should you and your ministry be interested in exploring becoming "trauma-informed," here are some points of connection I see between the 4-point definition of a trauma informed approach above, as well as a proposed ministry definition of the 6 key points. First, we will reframe the definition within the context of ministry.

A Trauma-Informed Ministry intentionally shapes a culture within their worshipping community that:

1. **Realizes** the widespread impact of trauma—those deeply distressing and emotional experiences that leave lasting effects—and provides practical ministry interventions as well as support for ongoing mental health interventions.

2. **Recognizes** the signs and symptoms of trauma in the children, youth, men and women it ministers to as well as the effects that living with a traumatized individual has on all relationships—marriage, family, work, and social.

3. **Responds** to the need within its worshipping community and the needs of its neighbors by fully integrating knowledge about trauma into church and ministry policies, procedures, and ministry practices. And,

4. Seeks to actively **resist re-traumatization** that can occur when appropriate recognition and intervention is not wed with compassion and a commitment to stabilizing relationships and supportive structures that destigmatize mental health issues.

Intrigued? Here are some questions for ministry that address the needed six key principles to a trauma-informed approach:

1. **Safety**: Not just physical safety, but emotional and relational safety as well. *Is there structure in place that allows for vulnerable people to feel included and protected within the worshipping community?*

2. **Trustworthiness and Transparency**: *Is authenticity a characteristic valued highly within your community of faith? Do those in ministry leadership appear as broken people in need of God's grace, just as those they minister to? Are confidences kept?*

3. **Peer support**: *Does the church go beyond being friendly to being a place someone can make friendships? Can a traumatized person find a listening ear and a welcome with others that are walking the same road to recovery, grace, and love of self and others? Can this happen both in large group and small group settings? Are ministry leaders modeling self-care through their personal practices?*

4. **Collaboration and mutuality**: *Does the church view its ministry to victimized people, traumatized individuals, and vulnerable children as integral to its call to Kingdom work for God or is it simply a niche ministry? Can the church work with others, even across ideological and denominational lines, for the betterment of hurting people?*

5. **Empowerment, voice and choice**: *Are those that are ministered to also given opportunity and empowered to minister within the church, understanding that they bring value and wisdom to the worshipping community? Are they fully integrated into the life of the church and given a voice for self-advocacy as well as outreach and mission?*

6. **Cultural, Historical, and Gender Issues**: *Does the church recognize the unique cultural issues sometimes bound up with trauma? Within the context of what has defined your worshipping community, is there room for the expression of faith and practice in ways that honor the unique cultural, historical, and gender backgrounds of those you seek to serve?*

As you can see, I have purposefully borrowed the structure and language of SAMHSA's definitions and guidelines so that a church hoping to become "trauma-informed" can speak the same language as those in the educational, mental health, medical or other fields also working to be trauma-informed. Purposefully seek out those within your church who can connect you to resources and expertise outside the church. As you build those bridges to those outside the church, you will help your ministry strengthen and grow!

Parting questions:

- **What is one thing that you learned today that can help you be more compassionate towards those that might be struggling with ACEs or trauma this week?**
- **Looking over the questions framed around the six key principles of a trauma-informed ministry above, which do you think your church could answer positively? Where do you see room for growth?**

Close in Prayer:

 "God our Comforter, Jesus our Advocate, Holy Spirit our intercessor—you care so deeply about us and the woundedness we carry with us each day. Help us see our weaknesses as strengths when we allow your light, love and grace to shine through us. Work on our hearts and our minds in this coming week to consider our role as advocates as we consider becoming a trauma-informed community of faith. Amen."

Week 3: Was Jesus' ministry "trauma-informed?"

Key idea: Jesus understood the devastating effects of trauma and adversity and his ministry was shaped in a way that responded to our needs.

Key verses:

- "'The Spirit of the Lord is on me,
    because he has anointed me
    to *proclaim good news to the poor*.
  He has sent me to *proclaim freedom for the prisoners*
    and recovery of sight for the blind,
  to *set the oppressed free*, to proclaim the year of the Lord's favor.'

  Then he rolled up the scroll, gave it back to the attendant and sat down. The eyes of everyone in the synagogue were fastened on him. He began by saying to them, 'Today this scripture is fulfilled in your hearing'" (Luke 4:17-21, NIV).

- "I have come that they might have life and have it to the full." –Jesus in John 10:10

Starting out:

- Go around the circle or table and introduce yourself by sharing the following:
    - your name,
    - an activity you engaged in this last week that gave you joy, and
    - something you are looking forward to today.

Open the study in prayer:

"Jesus, as we look to your example in ministry, open our hearts and minds for what it means to minister as you would—to our community, within this congregation, and on behalf of those who have experienced adversity and trauma. Keep us from the errors of either judgment or complacency as we learn to embody your love and grace to others. In your name we ask your blessing on this time. Amen."

From Chaplain Chris to the group:

(please read aloud, with a facilitator reading, or taking turns reading around the circle or table)

Last week the study focused on a growing trend in education, mental health, social services, and health care that has now extended to ministry settings: *becoming trauma-informed.*

Trauma results when we experience something as physically or emotionally harmful or life threatening. A traumatic event, circumstance or series of events leaves a lasting effect on our ability to experience "life to the full" as Jesus intended (John 10:10). Adversity, and particularly traumatic stress in childhood, leaves us scarred—affecting our mental, physical, social, emotional, and spiritual well-being. Trauma, adversity and toxic stress are profoundly individualized phenomena, as each individual internalizes difficult circumstances, including abuse and neglect, differently.

As a church seeking to help those who have experienced trauma, this insight should affect our approach in ministry and outreach. But how does a church avoid losing its focus on the gospel? Will being trauma-informed mean becoming just another social service agency?

These are good issues to wrestle through as a faith community. I know that for me, as a Christian, everything I encounter that purports to impact ministry is examined in light of two essential questions:

- FIRST… is it scriptural, and
- SECOND… can I see it as something Jesus would endorse?

These are important considerations if my ministry—if your local ministry—is to remain focused on its fundamental purpose and calling: to expand the Kingdom of God as embodied in Jesus' ministry. So, as we consider the import of the trauma-informed movement on our ministries, we must ask: *was Jesus and his ministry "trauma-informed?"*

Discuss:

- How have you seen traumatic experiences or adversity in your own life as a hurdle to experiencing life to its fullest? How has your faith in Jesus and relationship with God helped you through these difficulties in life?
- What do you think about Chaplain Chris' desire to explore whether or not Jesus' ministry was "trauma-informed?" How important is it to you that a ministry approach or program be grounded scripturally? How important is it that you feel it's something Jesus would endorse?

Read: Luke 4:14-21

[14] Jesus returned to Galilee in the power of the Spirit, and news about him spread through the whole countryside. [15] He was teaching in their synagogues, and everyone praised him.

[16] He went to Nazareth, where he had been brought up, and on the Sabbath day he went into the synagogue, as was his custom. He stood up to read, [17] and the scroll of the prophet Isaiah was handed to him. Unrolling it, he found the place where it is written:

[18] "The Spirit of the Lord is on me,
  because he has anointed me
  to proclaim good news to the poor.

He has sent me to proclaim freedom for the prisoners
    and recovery of sight for the blind,
to set the oppressed free,
 19   to proclaim the year of the Lord's favor."

 20 Then he rolled up the scroll, gave it back to the attendant and sat down. The eyes of everyone in the synagogue were fastened on him. 21 He began by saying to them, "Today this scripture is fulfilled in your hearing."

Discuss:

- Why do you think Jesus chose this passage for his "sermon" in his hometown synagogue? In what ways was the scripture "fulfilled" in their hearing that day as Jesus said, and in what ways do you see this passage still being fulfilled?

- What groups of people would hear Jesus' message and think it was particularly good news? Why? What groups might be resistant to Jesus' message for the poor and oppressed? Why might they resist the message?

 Applying science, applying the Word:

Please read aloud the following from Chaplain Chris...

Last time, I presented the framework provided by the Substance Abuse and Mental Health Services Administration as a way of explaining trauma-informed approaches to systems and organizations. Today, we begin to more closely examine this framework point by point in light of Jesus' ministry. We'll begin with the first identifier of a trauma-informed ministry: the realization of the widespread impact of trauma and potential paths for recovery.

In order to remind ourselves of the full context, I will reiterate the definition provided in my earlier lesson. According to the <u>Substance Abuse and Mental Health Services Administration (SAMHSA)</u>, "a program, organization, or system that is **trauma-informed**:

1. *Realizes* the widespread impact of trauma and understands potential paths for recovery;

2. *Recognizes* the signs and symptoms of trauma in clients, families, staff, and others involved with the system;

3. *Responds* by fully integrating knowledge about trauma into policies, procedures, and practices; and

4. Seeks to actively resist *re-traumatization*."

A trauma-informed approach to ministry starts with the realization of the widespread impact of trauma. Certainly, if a church or ministry is not aware or is in denial of the problem posed by adversity in childhood, toxic stress, and the effects of trauma on whose they minister too, it cannot properly address potential paths for recovery and healing.

I believe it can be shown that Jesus was trauma-informed through any and all of these points, but especially this first one. Jesus knew the tremendous brokenness of the world, and he knew the power of the Kingdom of God to address the needs of people traumatized by the evil of this world and the effects of sin. The first words spoken by Jesus as he began his ministry suggest this sensitivity and emphasis.

Those first words of Jesus?

> "The time has come... The Kingdom of God has come near. Repent and believe the good news" (Mark 1:15, NIV).

The announcement of Jesus to inaugurate and frame his ministry further expanded on this theme. Jesus had returned to Galilee after his baptism and testing in the wilderness. He entered the synagogue where he grew up, in his hometown of Nazareth. He stood up to read from the scroll of the prophet Isaiah, finding the place where it is written:

> "'The Spirit of the Lord is on me,
> because he has anointed me
> to *proclaim good news to the poor*.
> He has sent me to *proclaim freedom for the prisoners*
> and recovery of sight for the blind,
> to *set the oppressed free*, to proclaim the year of the Lord's favor.'
>
> Then he rolled up the scroll, gave it back to the attendant and sat down. The eyes of everyone in the synagogue were fastened on him. He began by saying to them, 'Today this scripture is fulfilled in your hearing'" (Luke 4:17-21).

These first two instances of Jesus' public preaching ministry show that he was, indeed, "trauma-informed" in the sense that he recognized the widespread impact of trauma and understood the paths to recovery!

I also love the balance that these two teachings contain. They help instruct what trauma-informed ministry would look like.

One shows the need for personal volition in the healing process, as the need to repent—to turn from—one way of living and relating to the world is emphasized.

The second shows that the "good news" of the Kingdom of God was centered in a redeeming work that goes beyond just personal salvation—it's a work that addresses the wrongs done to the poor, those who are imprisoned, and proclaims freedom to those under oppression.

This was a work that would be done through the Kingdom of God, as an expression of the Lord's favor, initiated by God for the benefit of all who turn to God for help.

Jesus recognized the tremendous need of those harassed and helpless who desperately needed good news, and compassionately engaged them in love. He gave not only of himself, ultimately to the point of death on the cross, but also pleaded with his followers to join him in meeting the need of a world traumatized by sin and the brokenness it produces in relationships.

As he said to his disciples then, he calls to us today, "The harvest is plentiful but the workers are few. Ask the Lord of the harvest, therefore, to send out workers into his harvest field" (Matthew 9:36-38).

Parting questions:

- **What from Chaplain Chris' discussion of Jesus' approach to ministry stood out to you?**
- **Who in your church or community do you think most needs to hear the compassionate words of Jesus expressed through a church that understands the widespread impact of trauma and potential paths to recovery? Where and how do you connect with these individuals?**

Close in Prayer:

 "God, thank you for sending Jesus Christ so we could see your love and compassion embodied in a person like us. Jesus, you came to bring a gospel of liberation and freedom from guilt and shame. For those in our midst that are being held captive because of their experience of trauma, use us to proclaim a message of hope. In your name, Lord. Amen."

Week 4: How the traumatized can look like they "have it all together."

Key idea: As we continue to explore the aspects of Jesus' ministry in light of trauma-informed principles, it is important to note that those dealing with trauma and adversity don't always look the same. Some may be leaders in their community, just like Nicodemus was. Adversity is not destiny, but trauma does leave its mark!

Key passage:

- ⁷ You should not be surprised at my saying, 'You must be born again.' ⁸ The wind blows wherever it pleases. You hear its sound, but you cannot tell where it comes from or where it is going. So it is with everyone born of the Spirit."

  ⁹ "How can this be?" Nicodemus asked. (John 3:7-9)

Starting out:

- Go around the circle or table and introduce yourself by sharing the following:
  - ○ your name,
  - ○ your favorite thing to eat for breakfast, and
  - ○ your most memorable birthday (and why it was the most memorable).

Open the study in prayer:

"Jesus, we ask for your wisdom and insight today. Holy Spirit, allow the words of Scripture to become alive to us so that we might see them in a new way today, applying the truths they contain to our present circumstance. Creator God, we are thankful that each and every person is here on earth for a purpose, and it is your purpose that they know and receive your profound love for them. In the name of the Father, Son, and Holy Spirit. Amen."

From Chaplain Chris to the group:

(please read aloud, with a facilitator reading, or taking turns reading around the circle or table)

We are now a month into our discussion of trauma-informed ministry, and if you are still here perhaps you agree with me that these concepts have the power to energize the church's mission and ministry? There is a growing body of evidence that suggests that if we can break the cycle of adversity in childhood the Church will help everyone experience "life to the full" as Jesus intended (John 10:10). That is GREAT news!

In previous studies we've seen Jesus' particular concern with the oppressed and those who lack hope in their present circumstance. Beyond simply asking that the "little children come unto him," Jesus is concerned with the conditions that persist in our culture that perpetuate childhood trauma (Luke 18:16).

While each person internalizes potentially traumatic experiences differently, and not all trauma equates to a life-time of difficulties, every society would be better off if it could alleviate childhood suffering, neglect, and abuse. Jesus made it clear where he stood in regards to protecting children from the evils of the world when he said it would be better off for someone to have "a large millstone hung around their neck and to be drowned in the depths of the sea" than to cause a child to stumble (Matthew 18:6).

While I particularly focus on a trauma-informed ministry approach when it comes to working with children, youth, and their families, these principles are transferrable to any population. I hope you you'll forgive my emphasis on children, because it is not only my area of ministry focus, but I sense it represents the church's best hope in alleviating suffering by breaking the generational cycle of adversity and traumatic experience.

Discuss:

- How could addressing the causes of childhood trauma break a generational cycle of harm that is passed from one generation to the next? How could your church focus on children in adversity while still becoming more compassionate to all traumatized individuals?
- Why do you think Jesus spoke so strongly about protecting children physically and spiritually?

Read: John 3:1-21 (NIV)

Now there was a Pharisee, a man named Nicodemus who was a member of the Jewish ruling council. [2] He came to Jesus at night and said, "Rabbi, we know that you are a teacher who has come from God. For no one could perform the signs you are doing if God were not with him."

[3] Jesus replied, "Very truly I tell you, no one can see the kingdom of God unless they are born again."

[4] "How can someone be born when they are old?" Nicodemus asked. "Surely they cannot enter a second time into their mother's womb to be born!"

[5] Jesus answered, "Very truly I tell you, no one can enter the kingdom of God unless they are born of water and the Spirit. [6] Flesh gives birth to flesh, but the Spirit gives birth to spirit. [7] You should not be surprised at my saying, 'You must be born again.' [8] The wind blows wherever it pleases. You hear its sound, but you cannot tell where it comes from or where it is going. So it is with everyone born of the Spirit."

[9] "How can this be?" Nicodemus asked.

[10] "You are Israel's teacher," said Jesus, "and do you not understand these things? [11] Very truly I tell you, we speak of what we know, and we testify to what we have seen, but still you people do not accept our testimony. [12] I have spoken to you of earthly things and you do not believe; how then will you believe if I speak of heavenly things? [13] No one has ever gone into heaven except the one who came from heaven—the Son of Man. [14] Just as Moses lifted up the snake in the wilderness, so the Son of Man must be lifted up, [15] that everyone who believes may have eternal life in him."

[16] For God so loved the world that he gave his one and only Son, that whoever believes in him shall not perish but have eternal life. [17] For God did not send his Son into the world to condemn the world, but to save the world through him. [18] Whoever believes in him is not condemned, but whoever does not believe stands condemned already because they have not believed in the name of God's one and only Son. [19] This is the verdict: Light has come into the world, but people loved darkness instead of light because their deeds were evil. [20] Everyone who does evil hates the light, and will not come into the light for fear that their deeds will be exposed. [21] But whoever lives by the truth comes into the light, so that it may be seen plainly that what they have done has been done in the sight of God. (John 3:1-21)

Discuss:

- Why do you think Nicodemus was drawn to meet with Jesus? With what tone and posture (attitude) do you imagine Nicodemus approaching Jesus? How does this affect the way you read Jesus' response?

- What do you like best about this story? What (if anything) troubles you about this passage?

 Applying science, applying the Word:

Please read aloud the following from Chaplain Chris…

Last week, we kept the focus on the first identifier of a trauma-informed ministry: the realization of the widespread impact of trauma and potential paths for recovery. This week we'll examine how Jesus recognized the signs and symptoms of trauma in those who appeared to "have it all together."

Jesus knew the tremendous brokenness of the world, and he knew the power of the Kingdom of Heaven to address the needs of people traumatized by the evil of this world and the effect of sin. Jesus could perceive the effects of this brokenness within everyone; therefore no one was disqualified from an encounter with the divine and an opportunity to embrace healing and wholeness.

To flesh out this dynamic in Jesus' ministry, we'll compare and contrast Jesus' interactions with the learned Nicodemus, a member of the Jewish ruling council, and the Samaritan woman at the well (you can find the full context of these stories in John's gospel, Chapter 3 and 4). Jesus understands that both Nicodemus and the Samaritan woman need something only he can offer, but his knowledge of their situation—his "recognition of the signs and symptoms" of trauma, if you will—shapes the way he interacts with them in turn. Because the gospel of John tells the story first of Nicodemus, I'll start there. (Next week we will address Jesus' interaction with the Samaritan woman).

There is a lot that can be said about this encounter between Nicodemus and Jesus, but for our purposes we will examine how Jesus responds to Nicodemus. Does Jesus recognize any "signs and symptoms" within Nicodemus that might point to trauma or any other adversity? Here are a few observances:

- Nicodemus is coming from a position of power and influence. He initiates the conversation.
- Nicodemus speaks first, complimenting Jesus. Nicodemus attributes Jesus' work to his having "come from God."
- Jesus responds by challenging Nicodemus, speaking of God's Kingdom and the need to be born again.
- Nicodemus, rather than admit his confusion, throws out an objection to Jesus' statement.
- Jesus recognizes Nicodemus' defensiveness as a signal that he is confused and surprised. Jesus asks Nicodemus to grasp something of spiritual significance rather than focusing on just the physical.
- Nicodemus releases some of his defensiveness by simply asking, "How can this be?" Clearly, any perceived power in this interaction has shifted from Nicodemus to Jesus.
- Jesus challenges Nicodemus' foundations on which he has built his self-identity: position, power, knowledge, and his ability as a "ruler" to judge.

What can be gleaned from this? Well, I'd like to point out that not all people walking around with trauma, or high "ACE" scores (adverse childhood experiences like abuse or neglect), are going to present as lowly or trouble-ridden! There are enough socially acceptable ways to cope with stress, even toxic stress, that we might first miss someone who has deep emotional pain in our faith community. Perfectionism, high standards and ideals, and worldly success often mask deep insecurities which have their root in unsettled feelings of shame and self-loathing.

Jesus' willingness to cut through all the fine theological discussion he might have had with Nicodemus (the proverbial *"how many angels can dance on the head of a pin?"* type of discussion) suggests that he is aware of spiritual and relational insecurities that can be masked by position and power.

Certainly, we have no way of knowing Nicodemus' childhood, but Jesus' insistence to discuss matters of the Spirit rather than focusing on the physical impossibility of being "born again" could indicate that he sees a deeper need within this nighttime visitor than mere intellectual enlightenment.

Before we end this lesson, I believe my conjecture regarding Nicodemus may gain a little more credibility if I take a moment to highlight a few specifics of the original ACE Study...

In the late 1990s, Dr. Vincent J. Felitti of the Department of Preventative Medicine, Southern California Permanente Medical Group (Kaiser Permanente) and Robert F. Anda of the National Center for Chronic Disease Prevention and Health Promotion, Centers for Disease Control and Prevention, conducted an epidemiological study that would soon simply be referred to as the "ACE study."

ACEs are adverse childhood experiences that harm children's developing brains so profoundly that the effects show up decades later and Felitti and Anda's research showed overwhelming correlation between adversity or trauma in childhood and the adult onset of chronic diseases, depression and other mental illness, violence and being a victim of violence.[2] Hundreds of scientific papers have verified and built upon the findings of the original ACE Study. The 10 ACEs Felitti and Anda measured were:

- Physical, sexual and verbal abuse.
- Physical and emotional neglect.
- Witnessing a mother being abused.
- Losing a parent to separation, divorce or other reason.
- A family member who is:
  - depressed or diagnosed with other mental illness;
  - addicted to alcohol or another substance;
  - in prison.
  - Witnessing a mother being abused.[3]

Quite a list, isn't it? Surely we can have compassion on those that experienced these difficulties in childhood. We might expect that these experiences are more common among some other group of people in much worse circumstances than we find ourselves.

Yet, our hopes would be misplaced and many of our expectations wrong. In fact, in the original ACE Study, "The mean age of the 8,506 persons… was 56.1 years (range 19-92 years); 52.1% were women; 79.4% were white. Forty-three percent had graduated from college; only 6.0% had not graduated from high school."[4]

These survey respondents, then, were predominantly white, middle class Americans (*they were all well enough off to have private insurance!*), reflecting the general make up of many of our nation's faith communities. The findings of the ACE Study were surprising to many, then, in that they showed a predominance of trauma in populations generally believed to be shielded from adversity by wealth, privilege, or circumstance.

The prevalence of ACEs in Montana bears out this truth: adversity affects a significant percentage of our population. Montana, out of all the states in which subsequent ACE surveys were completed, had the highest percentage of children living in a home with alcohol or substance abuse (19%), coinciding

---

[2] V.J. Felitti, Anda, R.F., Nordenberg, D., Williamson, D.F., Spitz, A.M., Edwards, V., & Koss, M. P. (1998) Relationship of childhood abuse and household dysfunction to many of the leading causes of death in adults: The Adverse Childhood Experiences (ACE) Study. American Journal of Preventive Medicine 14(4), 245-258.

[3] Felitti, et al., ibid.

[4] Ibid, 249.

with extremely high rates of economic hardship (28%) and divorce (26%).[5] This is my ministry context... statistics for your state can be found in the same study.

Among the findings of Montana's ACE survey, ChildTrends reported that 17% of children have experienced three or more ACEs, and 1 in 10 have four or more.[6] Early mortality rates increase greatly for those having four or more ACEs, as some studies suggest that those with this level or trauma and adversity in their lives die an average of twenty years earlier than those with no ACEs.[7]

Parting questions:

- **How does viewing Nicodemus as someone who might have experienced his own trauma affect the way you read John 3? Even if Nicodemus was not a trauma-survivor, how does Jesus' interaction with him reflect the values of a trauma-informed approach?**
- **What difference does it make that 10% of Montana's children have experienced four or more ACEs? Who in your community is working with children who have experienced adversity?**

Close in Prayer:

 "God, move us to see that every individual we encounter may be silently carrying a heavy load. For those children in Montana currently enduring adversity, we pray. For those in the church and in our community that are working through their own trauma history, we pray. May we be a place of support and grace for all those, who like Nicodemus, come looking for answers and hope. Amen."

---

[5] Vanessa Sacks, M.P.P., David Murphy, Ph.D. and Kristin Moore, Ph.D. "Adverse Childhood Experiences: National and State-Level Prevalence." ChildTrends Research Brief, July 2014; Publication #2014-28. 6.

[6] Ibid, 2.

[7] Carina Storrs, "Is Life Expectancy Reduced by a Traumatic Childhood?" ScientificAmerican.com, October 7, 2009. http://www.scientificamerican.com/article/childhood-adverse-event-life-expectancy-abuse-mortality/ (Accessed June 14, 2016).

Week 5: Does being trauma-informed mean we avoid saying hard things?

Key idea: Jesus was compassionate, yet firm. Jesus spoke the truth in love. Being trauma-informed means you prepare for the strong reaction some topics may elicit, not that you avoid all issues that may elicit a strong reaction.

Key verses:

- *"Give praise to the God and Father of our Lord Jesus Christ! He is the Father who gives tender love. All comfort comes from him. He comforts us in all our troubles. Now we can comfort others when they are troubled"* (2 Cor. 1:3-4, NIrV).
- *"God said to me, 'My grace is all you need. My power is strongest when you are weak.' So I am very happy to brag about how weak I am. Then Christ's power can rest on me'"* (2 Cor. 12:9).

Starting out:

- Go around the circle or table and introduce yourself by sharing the following:
  - your name,
  - something that comforted you as a child (a stuffed animal, a blanket, etc.) and who gave it to you or why it was special, and
  - something or someone who brings you comfort now when you are troubled.

Open the study in prayer:

"Jesus, today we will look at the way you said hard things to hurting people in a loving and compassionate way. We will admit that as we look around in our world, we see few examples of Jesus' masterful balance between truth and love, justice and compassion. God, we will need your help to even attempt to pattern our ministry after Jesus' example. Keep us, Spirit, from being so heavy-handed with our truths that we re-traumatize people. Keep us, too, from erring by mistaking compassion with condescension, denying those who need a message of hope the truth that will set them free. In your name. Amen."

From Chaplain Chris to the group:

(please read aloud, with a facilitator reading, or taking turns reading around the circle or table)

Last week we looked at Nicodemus' interaction with Jesus in John, chapter 3. Today, we'll continue the discussion of Jesus' ability to recognize the signs and symptoms of trauma, by comparing and contrasting that interaction with the one Jesus has with the Samaritan woman at the well in John's gospel, chapter 4.

One necessary note before looking again at the interaction between two people, Jesus and the Samaritan woman: the social environment of the time made it VERY unlikely that a Jewish man would have anything at all to do with a Samaritan woman, regardless of her personal reputation. The social, religious, and ethnic barriers between the two parties represented in this interaction would be difficult for us to replicate.

Embracing a trauma-informed ministry may just open your church or fellowship up to those that appear very different than you. It could stretch your comfort zone, but also open you up to a host of new friendships and relationships that you will find very rewarding.

Discuss:

- Who is your church unlikely to have any interaction with in your community? Why is this?
- Could embracing some of the values and approaches to ministry presented in this study over the last month help bridge the divide between your faith community and those that are presently unlikely to interact with you (and you with them)?

Read: John 4:4-42

⁴ Now he had to go through Samaria. ⁵ So he came to a town in Samaria called Sychar, near the plot of ground Jacob had given to his son Joseph. ⁶ Jacob's well was there, and Jesus, tired as he was from the journey, sat down by the well. It was about noon.

⁷ When a Samaritan woman came to draw water, Jesus said to her, "Will you give me a drink?" ⁸ (His disciples had gone into the town to buy food.)

⁹ The Samaritan woman said to him, "You are a Jew and I am a Samaritan woman. How can you ask me for a drink?" (For Jews do not associate with Samaritans.)

¹⁰ Jesus answered her, "If you knew the gift of God and who it is that asks you for a drink, you would have asked him and he would have given you living water."

¹¹ "Sir," the woman said, "you have nothing to draw with and the well is deep. Where can you get this living water? ¹² Are you greater than our father Jacob, who gave us the well and drank from it himself, as did also his sons and his livestock?"

¹³ Jesus answered, "Everyone who drinks this water will be thirsty again, ¹⁴ but whoever drinks the water I give them will never thirst. Indeed, the water I give them will become in them a spring of water welling up to eternal life."

¹⁵ The woman said to him, "Sir, give me this water so that I won't get thirsty and have to keep coming here to draw water."

¹⁶ He told her, "Go, call your husband and come back."

17 "I have no husband," she replied.

Jesus said to her, "You are right when you say you have no husband. 18 The fact is, you have had five husbands, and the man you now have is not your husband. What you have just said is quite true."

19 "Sir," the woman said, "I can see that you are a prophet. 20 Our ancestors worshiped on this mountain, but you Jews claim that the place where we must worship is in Jerusalem."

21 "Woman," Jesus replied, "believe me, a time is coming when you will worship the Father neither on this mountain nor in Jerusalem. 22 You Samaritans worship what you do not know; we worship what we do know, for salvation is from the Jews. 23 Yet a time is coming and has now come when the true worshipers will worship the Father in the Spirit and in truth, for they are the kind of worshipers the Father seeks. 24 God is spirit, and his worshipers must worship in the Spirit and in truth."

25 The woman said, "I know that Messiah" (called Christ) "is coming. When he comes, he will explain everything to us."

26 Then Jesus declared, "I, the one speaking to you—I am he."

The Disciples Rejoin Jesus

27 Just then his disciples returned and were surprised to find him talking with a woman. But no one asked, "What do you want?" or "Why are you talking with her?"

28 Then, leaving her water jar, the woman went back to the town and said to the people, 29 "Come, see a man who told me everything I ever did. Could this be the Messiah?" 30 They came out of the town and made their way toward him.

31 Meanwhile his disciples urged him, "Rabbi, eat something."

32 But he said to them, "I have food to eat that you know nothing about."

33 Then his disciples said to each other, "Could someone have brought him food?"

34 "My food," said Jesus, "is to do the will of him who sent me and to finish his work. 35 Don't you have a saying, 'It's still four months until harvest'? I tell you, open your eyes and look at the fields! They are ripe for harvest. 36 Even now the one who reaps draws a wage and harvests a crop for eternal life, so that the sower and the reaper may be glad together. 37 Thus the saying 'One sows and another reaps' is true. 38 I sent you to reap what you have not worked for. Others have done the hard work, and you have reaped the benefits of their labor."

Many Samaritans Believe

39 Many of the Samaritans from that town believed in him because of the woman's testimony, "He told me everything I ever did." 40 So when the Samaritans came to him, they urged him to stay with them, and he stayed two days. 41 And because of his words many more became believers.

42 They said to the woman, "We no longer believe just because of what you said; now we have heard for ourselves, and we know that this man really is the Savior of the world."

Discuss:

- Why do many of the Samaritans come to believe in Jesus as the Messiah? (verse 39-42)

- What role do Jesus' disciples play in this narrative? How do they come off looking by their words and behavior (especially in comparison to the Samaritan woman)?

Applying science, applying the Word:

Please read aloud the following from Chaplain Chris...

Last week we explored Jesus' interaction with Nicodemus in John 3. We discussed how trauma can sometimes be "disguised" by coping mechanisms that make it appear as though nothing is wrong, though the trauma experience still colors the attitudes and actions of the survivor. Today, our attention shifts to those who make it clear by their words and actions that they have experienced heartache, trauma, and adversity.

Considering Jesus' interaction with the Samaritan woman in light of trauma-informed principles, here are a few observations:

- Jesus initiates the discussion and takes the first step in bridging the wide social, ethnic, and religious divide between them.
- The woman is taken aback, and responds in her surprise... asking, "Aren't you breaking your own rules to ask me for a drink?"
- Jesus, like with Nicodemus, has no real interest in focusing on the physical realities of this chance encounter. He would much rather speak of spiritual matters. He brings up her need to ask him for a drink of "living water."
- Like Nicodemus, the Samaritan woman seems unable to comprehend the significance of what Jesus is saying. So, like Nicodemus, her response sounds defensive. She points to Jesus' lack of an instrument to retrieve water. She points to her own ethnic heritage (a daughter of Jacob) and the connection to the physical well they stood over. She challenges Jesus' authority and importance.
- Jesus side steps the woman's defensiveness and offers a gift, eternal life. He offers an end to her spiritual thirst.
- The woman responds positively, seeing a way to meet her personal need. She asks for what Jesus is offering.
- Jesus asks her to go and get her husband, to which she replies that she has no husband. Jesus then points out that she is right in this statement, only because she is merely living with the man without being wed, and that five previous times she has been married (and, presumably, divorced).
- Having established his credibility, Jesus asks the woman to believe in him and gives her an opportunity to respond by focusing on spiritual realities and a future hope that can start for her as soon as she decides ("a new time is coming. In fact, it is already here..." in verse 23).

- The Samaritan woman believes in Jesus, gets a "new start," and becomes a powerful messenger. Many believe in Jesus because of her words, and many more believe because they accept her invitation to come listen to him and hear for themselves (verses 39-42).

What can be gleaned from this interaction? Was Jesus' conversation with the Samaritan woman "trauma-informed?" Would becoming trauma-informed as a ministry mean you could no longer identify sin and suggest righteousness (living in right relationship with God through obedience and discipleship) as a means of spiritual, emotional, and relational healing?

Clearly, Jesus' initiative in reaching out and expressing a need that the Samaritan woman might meet was counter-cultural. I happen to believe it was also trauma-informed. The woman clearly was living on the fringes of an already marginalized people group… she came alone to the well in the heat of the day, either avoiding the women who would come at the start of the day or unwelcome in their midst. Her defensiveness, like Nicodemus' response in the previous chapter (John 3), suggests that she is used to being on her own with little or no support system or advocacy on her behalf by others. Jesus' speaking to her and asking her for a drink suggests to her that her marginalization is NOT going to be an issue for him. He sees her value, even if she does not.

Furthermore, while some might see some pointedness and crudeness in the way Jesus "reveals" her shortcomings—"you are right to say you have no husband… in fact you have had five husbands"—I see a willingness by Jesus to address a symptom of her trauma, identify it in a factual but nonjudgmental way, before getting on to more weighty matters. I think the evidence of Jesus' tone can be seen in how the woman responds. Had there been judgment or condemnation in Jesus' voice, I doubt the conversation would have continued! Yet look at her response—she leaves to go and tell all of those in the village that she has found the Messiah!

Often those that have been most deeply wounded and ostracized can be the best agents of healing and reconciliation in a community. Jesus saw this trauma-informed aspect of ministry, and rather than using her as a means for his glory, leaving her at the well as he parades into town, he sends her forth to be the bearer of good news… God is near! The Messiah has come! Written off by many of her peers, Jesus writes her in to the story of Sychar's eternal destiny, placing her in a prominent role: "Many of the Samaritans from the town of Sychar believed in Jesus. They believed because of what the woman had said about him" (John 4:39).

I believe in the ministry maxim: people who feel broken are best reached by other people that have come to terms with their brokenness and need for God. In Alcoholics Anonymous, it's the former drunk that sponsors the newly initiated in the program, *not the teetotaler who has never had a sip!* Those already convicted of their sin and broken condition will steer clear of the self-righteous.

Those who have experienced trauma themselves have a tremendous gift in reaching others working through the effects of their traumatization. Indeed: people experiencing adversity and trauma are best reached by others who have also experienced trauma while embracing a faith-filled relationship with God. Here's the amazing thing, whether those in our ministries realize it or not: **we all have experienced brokenness.** Furthermore, we minister most powerfully out of the areas of our brokenness, not from our perceived strengths. As the Apostle Paul wrote:

"Give praise to the God and Father of our Lord Jesus Christ! He is the Father who gives tender love. All comfort comes from him. He comforts us in all our troubles. Now we can comfort others when they are troubled" (2 Cor. 1:3-4, NIrV).

"God said to me, 'My grace is all you need. My power is strongest when you are weak.' So I am very happy to brag about how weak I am. Then Christ's power can rest on me'" (2 Cor. 12:9).

I absolutely believe Jesus' ministry was "trauma-informed!" But, in seeing those affected by traumatic experience, beaten down and harassed by the weight of the adversity in their lives, he didn't see the trauma... he saw them. Each and every one of them as individuals worthy of a place in God's Kingdom.

As our ministries gain in skills and ability to recognize the symptoms and effects of trauma and childhood adversity, we must be careful not to make anyone a "project" or merely the focus of our charity. This was NOT Jesus' approach... the Samaritan woman didn't need to "work through her issues" before being commissioned as a minister of the gospel! Jesus needed her specifically because she had "issues!" Amazing... and how like the love and grace of God to take our imperfections and use them for his perfect purpose.

Parting questions:

- **How do you feel about the way Jesus exposed the Samaritan woman's need? Was he simply using the exercise of his power to "put her in her place," or was he speaking the truth in love? How would you feel in her position?**
- **Who has ministered to you out of a place of brokenness and humility? What difference does this make in ministry?**

Close in Prayer:

"God, it is true that you shine most brightly through the broken areas of our lives. As we seek to be more trauma-informed, both for our sakes and for those in our community, help us see that we can glory in our weakness, just as Paul did. When we embrace the brokenness in our lives, when we assume the way of the cross as necessary to our discipleship, we know we will see you move in our midst, Holy Spirit. Help us trust you, not only with our strengths and our abilities, Jesus, but also with our hurts, our trauma, and our pain. Amen."

Week 6: Responding to trauma within the compassionate Kingdom of God

Key idea: God's Kingdom stands apart from this world's kingdoms, bringing justice and mercy where trauma and heartache have prevailed.

Key verses:

- "My kingdom is not of this world..." –Jesus to Pilate in John 18:36
- Finally, be strong in the Lord and in his mighty power. [11] Put on the full armor of God, so that you can take your stand against the devil's schemes. [12] For our struggle is not against flesh and blood, but against the rulers, against the authorities, against the powers of this dark world and against the spiritual forces of evil in the heavenly realms. (Ephesians 6:10-12, NIV)

Starting out:

- Go around the circle or table and introduce yourself by sharing the following:
  - your name,
  - something you appreciate about the person on your left.

Open the study in prayer:

"God, you intend for us to live in a way that honors your place in our lives and embodies the character of your Son, Jesus Christ. As we consider the Kingdom of God, ushered in by Jesus' ministry nearly two thousand years ago, help us reflect the values of that kingdom in our church and ways of being community together. In the name of the Father, Son, and Holy Spirit. Amen."

From Chaplain Chris to the group:

(please read aloud, with a facilitator reading, or taking turns reading around the circle or table)

A trauma-informed approach to ministry starts with the realization of the widespread impact of trauma. Certainly, if a church or ministry is not aware or is in denial of the problem posed by adversity in childhood, toxic stress, and the effects of trauma on whose they minister too, it cannot properly address potential paths for recovery and healing.

Secondly, churches and faith-communities seeking to be trauma-informed will be constantly growing in their ability to recognize the signs and symptoms of trauma in those they minister to.

The next critical step is application—examining policies, procedures, and practices within the church. Those who comprise a system—whether that system is the church, a community, or a school—must turn a critical eye towards the ways that system may be causing or perpetuating trauma. Systems, communities, governments, denominations... basically any way of being connected in life together... these entities take on a life of their own.

When left unexamined in light of God's Word, these systems can be damaging and hurtful, perpetuating trauma and leaving people in their wake. Perhaps this is one way in which Christians can realize that their "battle" in becoming trauma-informed is "not against flesh and blood." Put another way, the battle is not against the individuals that make up a system that perpetuates trauma, **but against the system itself** for the sake of those caught up in it.

This work takes a great deal of discernment and can only truly be done in community with others also seeking to reform a system or community. This is a necessary step that takes the insights gained from increased knowledge and awareness and puts it into practice. That practice—moving towards a trauma-informed church and community—is what is suggested in points #3 and #4 of SAMHSA's guidelines for a trauma-informed system.

In order to remind ourselves of the full context, I will reiterate the definition provided in earlier lessons. According to the <u>Substance Abuse and Mental Health Services Administration (SAMHSA),</u> the concept of a trauma-informed approach would mean that "a program, organization, or system that is trauma-informed:

1. *Realizes* the widespread impact of trauma and understands potential paths for recovery;

2. *Recognizes* the signs and symptoms of trauma in clients, families, staff, and others involved with the system;

3. *Responds* by fully integrating knowledge about trauma into policies, procedures, and practices; and

4. Seeks to actively resist *re-traumatization*."

A church that seeks to be trauma-informed would be well served to consider the values of the Kingdom of God and ask: "Are these values reflected in our organization's policies, procedures, and practices?" As members of the church recognize the ways trauma can be perpetuated within systems and organizations, they may look to the other organizations and groups they belong to and carry those Kingdom principles over into businesses, schools, and social organizations. Together, groups of Christians in community can bring a great deal of reform, healing, and hope to those being harmed by systems that currently perpetuate trauma.

Discuss:

- As we turn our hearts and minds to the practical implications of the knowledge and insight gained through this series, are there things that you have experienced or observed in your church or community that might need to change? If a specific example comes to mind, share it with the group as well as how you see it fitting in with your understanding of becoming "trauma-informed." (Remember, healing/reforming systems is our goal, and so calling out individuals will not be helpful! Please, no names or name calling).

Read: John 18:33-37 (NIV)

³³ Pilate then went back inside the palace, summoned Jesus and asked him, "Are you the king of the Jews?"

³⁴ "Is that your own idea," Jesus asked, "or did others talk to you about me?"

³⁵ "Am I a Jew?" Pilate replied. "Your own people and chief priests handed you over to me. What is it you have done?"

³⁶ Jesus said, "My kingdom is not of this world. If it were, my servants would fight to prevent my arrest by the Jewish leaders. But now my kingdom is from another place."

³⁷ "You are a king, then!" said Pilate.

Jesus answered, "You say that I am a king. In fact, the reason I was born and came into the world is to testify to the truth. Everyone on the side of truth listens to me." (John 18:33-37)

Discuss:

- Why does Pilate seem to be confused/bewildered by Jesus? What do you think Pilate was expecting from Jesus?

- What evidence does Jesus give to Pilate that his kingdom is not "of this world?" What insight might this give us as we seek to reform systems and communities in order to be more trauma-informed?

Applying science, applying the Word:

Please read aloud the following from Chaplain Chris…

Jesus knew the tremendous brokenness of the world, and he knew the power of the Kingdom of Heaven to address the needs of people traumatized by the evil of this world and the effect of sin. Jesus' understanding of the fundamental failings of most human systems is clear in his critiques of both the religious establishment of his day as well as the Roman political and military complex. But rather than just point out the failings of the system, Jesus suggested that a new system could be put in place that would result in the justice, equity, and safety that any trauma-informed society would want to emulate.

Therefore, while multiple books could be written on this subject, I want to address the third way in which I observe that Jesus' ministry was trauma-informed: Jesus sought to respond to the hurt and damage that trauma had caused in the world by fully integrating knowledge about trauma into an alternative way of social organization- a "Kingdom of Heaven." This present and future kingdom would be governed by policies, procedures, and practices that would reflect the principles of a trauma-informed organization.

These principles are:

- Safety: physically and psychologically
- Trustworthiness and transparency that builds trust and maintains compassionate connection

- Peer support and mutual self-help
- Collaboration and community that results in a levelling of power differences between those served and those serving
- Providing opportunities for voice and meaningful choice
- Individuality and uniqueness is honored—each one an individual, not a project or a category
- Raises and addresses cultural, historical, and gender issues

In order to portray Jesus as forming a trauma-informed alternative to existing "kingdoms" in his day, we'll limit our focus to one passage of particular importance: Jesus' interaction with Pilate in John 18:33-37,

> *33 Pilate then went back inside the palace, summoned Jesus and asked him, "Are you the king of the Jews?"*
>
> *34 "Is that your own idea," Jesus asked, "or did others talk to you about me?"*
>
> *35 "Am I a Jew?" Pilate replied. "Your own people and chief priests handed you over to me. What is it you have done?"*
>
> *36 Jesus said, "My kingdom is not of this world. If it were, my servants would fight to prevent my arrest by the Jewish leaders. But now my kingdom is from another place."*
>
> *37 "You are a king, then!" said Pilate.*
>
> *Jesus answered, "You say that I am a king. In fact, the reason I was born and came into the world is to testify to the truth. Everyone on the side of truth listens to me." (John 18:33-37)*

Pilate, the fifth prefect of the province of Judaea, embodies the military and political might of the Roman Empire. He is familiar with the way that Rome governs—imposing "peace" through overwhelming military strength. Pilate, by nature of his position, was also familiar with the other significant rule in place over Judaea, the religious ruling and governing class represented by the Chief Priest, Caiaphas, and the Sanhedrin—70 men who formed a supreme council, or court, in ancient Israel. These were the two main "kingdoms" in place that Jesus posed a threat to.

When questioned about his position in regards to these kingdoms, Jesus tells Pilate, "My kingdom is not of this world" (verse 36). Throughout Jesus' ministry, he has focused on what the kingdom is or what is like. Here, before the Roman authority, Jesus focuses on how the Kingdom of God differs: it will not use force or intimidation. It is a Kingdom that speaks on behalf of truth and truthfulness, and those who recognize that truth listen and respond in kind. Absent is any form of coercion: physical, emotional or spiritual.

Jesus represented a compassionate call to align with a new and alternative "kingdom." This principle of non-violence in the face of oppression was as radical then as it is today. Jesus understood that any peace enforced by the threat of violence would never provide the sense of safety and security the human soul longs for. Jesus is completely transparent and trustworthy, a leader of integrity that guides his followers by his example and willingness to sacrifice position and power to place himself in the role of servant and messenger of the truth. In this way, Jesus serves as the ultimate example of one who created a community where power was shared equally and equitably. Jesus gave a voice to those without a voice—the marginalized and the overlooked. His desire to build an inclusive and accepting community placed him in the crosshairs of the religious elite, those who would label him a "friend of sinners" (Matthew 11:19). Jesus raised cultural, historical and gender issues that still reverberate through the church two thousand years later!

One may argue how well the Church exhibits the qualities of the compassionate Kingdom of God that Jesus ushered in with his ministry, but that fault lies with us—Jesus' followers—and not with his teaching or personal example.

Parting questions:

- **In what ways has the Church adopted the principles, procedures, and practices of this world—for better or worse? How could these ways of being community together be examined in light of God's Kingdom principles and a desire to be trauma-sensitive?**
- **Name one way that you see your church or community embodying the compassionate Kingdom of God. How can you build on this strength to reach those currently outside your fellowship?**

Close in Prayer:

"God, Jesus taught us to pray—Your Kingdom come; Your will be done, on earth as it is in heaven. This would be our desire. If we seek to become trauma-informed without considering the character of your Kingdom and its values, we'll simply replace one broken system for another. As much as possible, and by your grace and empowerment, help our community live up to your vision for your Church and your followers. In your name, and with your leading, we pray. Amen."

<u>Week 7: The weight we carry – how trauma and adversity affects adults</u>

Key idea: We carry the wounds of childhood into our adulthood, and recovery and building resilience requires we seek healing for old wounds

Key verses:

- "You intended to harm me, but God intended it for good to accomplish what is now being done, the saving of many lives." –Joseph to his brothers (Genesis 50:20, NIV)
- "[8] Three times I pleaded with the Lord to take it away from me. [9] But he said to me, 'My grace is sufficient for you, for my power is made perfect in weakness.' Therefore I will boast all the more gladly about my weaknesses, so that Christ's power may rest on me. [10] That is why, for Christ's sake, I delight in weaknesses, in insults, in hardships, in persecutions, in difficulties. For when I am weak, then I am strong." –Paul, speaking of his ongoing struggles and God's grace (2 Corinthians 12:8-10, NIV)

Starting out:

- Go around the circle or table and introduce yourself by sharing the following:
  - your name,
  - an experience you had as a child that has shaped your character as an adult.

Open the study in prayer:

"God, you are in the business of redeeming people and bringing good out of what others intend for harm. You walk with us in the valley experiences of our lives and we trust your promise that you never leave us nor forsake us. If we are honest, Lord, there have been many times we echoed the Psalmist's words—'how long, O Lord?'—and yet we know that your love remains. Help us to be patient with ourselves, patient in our sufferings, and reliant on your provision in the midst of trials and difficulty. In Jesus' Name. Amen."

From Chaplain Chris to the group:

(please read aloud, with a facilitator reading, or taking turns reading around the circle or table)

A fair amount of this study has focused on childhood trauma, as combatting the forces that injure and harm children in our communities may be the Church's best opportunity to make a Kingdom difference in this world. That does not mean, however, that it is only to addressing childhood trauma that God may be calling you as a church into trauma-informed ministry.

Since the first edition of this curriculum was published in 2017, I have heard from many people representing a wide spectrum of ministry initiatives focused on traumatized adults. As we learned in previous lessons, adults dealing with the effects of their trauma manifest those traumatic experiences in any number of ways. They don't always fit in to the neat boxes discussed within this curriculum—either the open woundedness and defensiveness of the Samaritan Woman or the stubborn pride of the perfectionist Pharisee, Nicodemus—and this is one of the great lessons taught us by the initial ACE Study! 17,000+ adults surveyed, and a staggering number of them had experienced tremendous adversity in childhood. Yet, here they were years and even decades later, functioning at a high enough level in society to have a steady job and good health insurance (as members of Kaiser Permanente's San Diego area clinics).[8]

My own ministry experience affirms this truth: time does NOT heal all wounds, especially childhood trauma. Not long ago, I was given the opportunity to write an article for the *Independent Record*, and I chose to write on the difficult of ministering to those who are shame-based in their thinking. Two weeks after the paper came out, a man well into his retirement years approached me and talked about his desire to end his life and put his grief and pain behind him. He had been a success as a man who poured himself into his work, but now he was depressed and suicidal as he neared his 80th birthday. The trauma he endured seven decades earlier, suppressed for so long, was as if it were only yesterday!

I was able to find this gentleman help with a local therapist and friend who is skilled in bringing healing to the relational and spiritual wounds this man had endured in childhood. Having endured his pain for 70 years, he now had the opportunity to find healing and the truth of God's Word as Paul related his own struggle with a "thorn in his flesh":

> *"[8] Three times I pleaded with the Lord to take it away from me. [9] But he said to me, 'My grace is sufficient for you, for my power is made perfect in weakness.' Therefore I will boast all the more gladly about my weaknesses, so that Christ's power may rest on me. [10] That is why, for Christ's sake, I delight in weaknesses, in insults, in hardships, in persecutions, in difficulties. For when I am weak, then I am strong."* (2 Corinthians 12:8-10, NIV)

God can do a wonderful thing through our weaknesses and pain, when we don't lose hope. We need a community of believers that will support us as we work through the issues related to trauma and its impact in our lives.

Beyond these individual examples, many churches and denominations are doing incredible work in trauma-related fields from domestic violence and human trafficking to disaster relief. I would hope that no matter where you feel called as a congregation or fellowship, you could see the opportunity presented through educating yourselves in the trauma-informed principles expounded upon in this study. Before we look at an example from scripture of the link between childhood and adult trauma, take a moment to reflect on your own experiences and discuss where you feel God may be calling you to examine the ministries you have to adults in light of trauma-informed ministry principles.

---

[8] "The Adverse Childhood Experiences Study – the Largest Public Health Study You Never Heard Of" by Jane Ellen Stevens. https://www.huffingtonpost.com/jane-ellen-stevens/the-adverse-childhood-exp_1_b_1943647.html

Discuss:

- Why might it be helpful to remember God's admonition to Paul (*'My grace is sufficient for you, for my power is made perfect in weakness.'*) when we seek to make our adult ministries trauma-informed?
- If your church has a recovery program, AA group, homeless ministry, or is involved in disaster relief, how might trauma-informed principles be applied to ensuring that those who are a part of these ministries would also feel welcome on Sunday mornings or in any other aspect of your life together as a church?

Read: Genesis 45:1-11; 50:15-21 (NIV)

Joseph Makes Himself Known

[1]Then Joseph could no longer control himself before all his attendants, and he cried out, "Have everyone leave my presence!" So there was no one with Joseph when he made himself known to his brothers. [2]And he wept so loudly that the Egyptians heard him, and Pharaoh's household heard about it.

[3]Joseph said to his brothers, "I am Joseph! Is my father still living?" But his brothers were not able to answer him, because they were terrified at his presence.

[4]Then Joseph said to his brothers, "Come close to me." When they had done so, he said, "I am your brother Joseph, the one you sold into Egypt! [5]And now, do not be distressed and do not be angry with yourselves for selling me here, because it was to save lives that God sent me ahead of you. [6]For two years now there has been famine in the land, and for the next five years there will be no plowing and reaping. [7]But God sent me ahead of you to preserve for you a remnant on earth and to save your lives by a great deliverance.

[8]"So then, it was not you who sent me here, but God. He made me father to Pharaoh, lord of his entire household and ruler of all Egypt. [9]Now hurry back to my father and say to him, 'This is what your son Joseph says: God has made me lord of all Egypt. Come down to me; don't delay. [10]You shall live in the region of Goshen and be near me—you, your children and grandchildren, your flocks and herds, and all you have. [11]I will provide for you there, because five years of famine are still to come. Otherwise you and your household and all who belong to you will become destitute.'

* * * * * * * * * *

Joseph Reassures His Brothers

[15]When Joseph's brothers saw that their father was dead, they said, "What if Joseph holds a grudge against us and pays us back for all the wrongs we did to him?" [16]So they sent word to Joseph, saying, "Your father left these instructions before he died: [17]'This is what you are to say to Joseph: I ask you to forgive your brothers the sins and the wrongs they committed in treating you so badly.' Now please

forgive the sins of the servants of the God of your father." When their message came to him, Joseph wept.

¹⁸ His brothers then came and threw themselves down before him. "We are your slaves," they said.

¹⁹ But Joseph said to them, "Don't be afraid. Am I in the place of God? ²⁰ You intended to harm me, but God intended it for good to accomplish what is now being done, the saving of many lives. ²¹ So then, don't be afraid. I will provide for you and your children." And he reassured them and spoke kindly to them.

Discuss:

- What does Joseph say to reassure his brothers? Does Joseph's trust that his traumatic childhood experiences were part of God's intention to "accomplish... the saving of many lives" provide us any insight into how we could address our own trauma? What role might forgiveness play in healing trauma?

- Does believing that God may bring about good from evil—harm done to children, especially—fit into a trauma-informed approach to ministry?

- When addressing the suffering in adults who have endured or are currently working through trauma, how can we validate their pain while also expressing hope that God is with them in the midst of their struggle?

Applying science, applying the Word:

Please read aloud the following from Chaplain Chris...

We see how Paul dealt with the unresolved struggles in his own life when he states:

"I was given a thorn in my flesh, a messenger of Satan, to torment me. ⁸ Three times I pleaded with the Lord to take it away from me. ⁹ But he said to me, 'My grace is sufficient for you, for my power is made perfect in weakness.' Therefore I will boast all the more gladly about my weaknesses, so that Christ's power may rest on me. ¹⁰ That is why, for Christ's sake, I delight in weaknesses, in insults, in hardships, in persecutions, in difficulties. For when I am weak, then I am strong." (2 Corinthians 12:7b-10)

I can recognize now after many years of processing, reflection, and prayer, that God was able to express a strength through my weaknesses and build a stronger character within me through some of the traumatic experiences I went through. I would think that many reading this could also see where God has built a certain strength or resolve within an area of hurt, woundedness, or pain. This is not simply the worldly wisdom expressed in the popular saying, "what doesn't kill you only makes you stronger," but a wisdom that comes through suffering and an insight gained into what really matters to you that rarely comes from a life of ease.

There is a phenomenon referred to as "Post-Traumatic Growth Syndrome." First studied in the 1990s, psychologists have been attempting to define what it is about the difficult process of recovery from a traumatic event that challenges a person's core beliefs that can leave a person more resilient, and sometimes even thankful for the "gift" they have received in seeing the world more clearly after their traumatic experience.

To evaluate the extent to which someone has achieved this kind of growth after trauma, psychologists often use various self-reporting surveys and scales. One such survey is called the Post-Traumatic Growth Inventory (PGTI) and was developed by Tedeschi and Calhoun, which they first reported on in the *Journal of Traumatic Stress* (1996 Jul; 9(3):455-71). They sought to measure positive responses in five key areas that they believed would show post-traumatic growth:

- Appreciation of life

- Relationships with others

- New possibilities in life

- Personal strength

- Spiritual change or renewal

I believe that you can likely perceive how going through a life-threatening, traumatic experience, and coming out the "other side" might impact each of these areas.

Pain, such as that experienced by Paul (referenced in the Bible passage earlier), has a way of focusing our thoughts and actions on what is truly important and lasting. For Joseph, his ordeal could have made him angry and resentful toward his brothers, but it didn't. Instead, it made him long for family and relationship even more.

The role a church or fellowship can play in helping those in the midst of their own pain and traumatic experience is to hold out hope for them that they, too, can experience a sense of growth as God redeems even their suffering. The beauty of the Christian story is that we are all part of a much larger narrative, and we can walk with one another through the most difficult struggles and provide companionship that makes the journey a little easier to endure.

Parting questions:

- **What is the most helpful thing someone has said or done for you when you were in the midst of suffering, a traumatic experience, or seeking to recover from something truly horrible and life-altering? Conversely, what was not helpful? How can our experiences help shape a plan for ministry to others that would be trauma-informed?**
- **How have you seen or experienced the phenomenon of "Post-Traumatic Growth" in your life or in the lives of those close to you? How has that "growth" shaped your character and ministry?**

Close in Prayer:

"Jesus, we know that you are well acquainted with suffering—both your own and the suffering of those of us you care so deeply for—and it compels your Spirit forward in ministry. Forgive us for the times when our own suffering has drawn us inward and caused us to retreat from your calling. Redeem our pain for your purpose and help us help. May our ministry to ALL—young and old—be informed by our growing knowledge of trauma-informed ministry principles so we can express your loving compassion to a hurting world. In your name, we pray. Amen."

Week 8: Now what do we do? A process for implementation

Key idea: Together the Spirit has drawn your group together, and together the Spirit will speak to you as you discern the "next steps" in trauma-informed ministry

Key verses:

- "Don't begin until you count the cost..." Jesus on discipleship in Luke 14:28
- "Dear children, let us not love with words or speech but with actions and in truth." 1 John 3:18

Starting out:

- Go around the circle or table and introduce yourself by sharing the following:
  - your name,
  - a time when you were sure that your church or fellowship was doing exactly what God wanted you to do.

Open the study in prayer:

"Holy Spirit, you have been a part of each of our gatherings and have heard our thoughts and questions about where you might lead us as we consider trauma-informed ministry. Help us to know what you are calling us to and to discern those first steps in compassionately and thoughtfully caring for those affected by adversity and trauma. You bring healing and hope through your people, and that would be our desire. Help us as we seek to help others. Amen."

From Chaplain Chris to the group:

(please read aloud, with a facilitator reading, or taking turns reading around the circle or table)

One major question that people have after a training on trauma or adverse childhood experiences and the impact they have on individuals, families, and communities is, "Okay, but what should we do?"

I appreciate the desire to have answers to very practical questions like these. The difficulty I have in answering this question is that any number of factors go into adequately answering the "what do we do next?" question. I hope by way of explanation, I can address some of these concerns while still giving a somewhat satisfactory answer.

First, there is the issue of contextualization. My primary ministry setting is with children in residential care. Secondarily, it's as a ministry leader in a small church in what passes as a city in Montana. The churches I hope to impress with the message of trauma-informed ministry principles are small and rural. Furthermore, Montana has a mental health crisis—specifically children growing up in a home where a care giver has a significant mental health diagnosis—as well as a problem with substance abuse and suicide. These are the topics that usually come to the foreground when talking with ministries in Montana about trauma-informed ministry. That is OUR context. YOUR ministry context will have some similarities as well as some significant differences. Recently, this curriculum was ordered by a school district in Hawaii in an effort to reach out to churches there that wanted to apply trauma-informed principles to their congregations and communities after natural disaster. Others have implemented the study in the context of a women's shelter and a soup kitchen ministering to the homeless. Each setting will implement trauma-informed principles differently.

At the conclusion of this week's study there are some questions that utilize SAMHSA's principles of a trauma-informed organization and expand upon those principles with questions designed to help you apply them to your ministry setting. Having gone through this curriculum, Capital Baptist Church in Annandale, Virginia, started a Trauma-Informed Care Ministry with the purpose of specifically coming alongside those that had experienced significant trauma or are currently going through a traumatic situation (http://capitalbaptist.org/careministry/). Care ministry leaders have been designated for both men and women so there can be a "point person" to approach with any needs or concerns. They put information on their website and produced a tri-fold brochure that is made available to the church as they launched the ministry in the fall of 2018 (see picture).

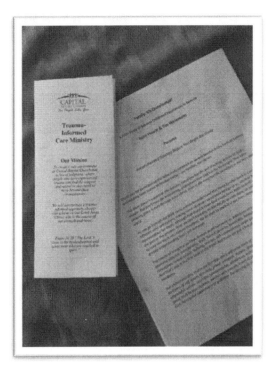

Rene Howitt, of Cope24: Changing our Parenting Experience, first engaged these materials you are reading in the spring of 2017. She was inspired to partner with Pastor Tim Wesemann to use her own expertise in speaking on Parenting and Adverse Childhood Experiences to create a Bible study on Genesis, called "Family: It's Complicated" (https://cope24.com/faith-based-church-initiative/). As someone who previewed those materials as they were being prepared, I can recommend them highly! Perhaps going through such a study would be a way to further engage your church or fellowship in integrating trauma-informed principles in your context.

Secondly, I have an absolute belief that the Spirit speaks to the Church, and can and wants to bring healing to traumatized individuals through you! I trust that, even now, there are some in your group who are being stirred in their spirit to put into practice some of what you have learned together. The wonderful thing about a message from the Spirit is that it can be confirmed by others as you share your passion. Perhaps the next step is simply to take a larger group through this study and open more hearts and minds to what might be done (Remember: the first aspect of becoming trauma-informed is REALIZING the wide-spread impact of trauma and that takes a commitment to educate others!). Perhaps the pastors or elders at your church need to be encouraged to learn about trauma and how it has and is affecting those in your community? So, the next step could be that you simply take what you have learned and present it to others. Many churches choose to use the "Paper Tigers" movie included with the curriculum to raise awareness and interest in ACEs, trauma, and how we can help youth be more resilient.

Lastly, because I TRULY believe in the previous point—the Spirit actively speaks to the church—I believe in discernment and decision-making practices that engage as wide an audience as possible. Holding a workshop that is based on collaboration and asking questions similar to those at the close of this study may be helpful. One approach, based on the "World Café" model[9], would ask that the group taking this study craft 3 or 4 questions that pertain to trauma-informed ministry which are discussed by small groups (4-5 people) at tables, with those individuals at tables being shuffled around a bit for each question so everyone gets to interact with everyone else. A "Graphic Recorder" asks for each group to report their insights after each round, or question, and writes (or draws!) something that remains in front of the group throughout the workshop. I love this approach because it focuses discussion while also making room for some of the quieter or often marginalized voices to be heard as part of the discernment process.

A similar process to this World Café model is one called "Appreciative Inquiry."[10] Again, questions are crafted by a group of people (likely those of you who have participated in this study) and then that group goes out and interviews representative members of the congregation or fellowship to gather feedback. The wonderful thing about Appreciative Inquiry, in my opinion, is that it looks to build upon those things that your community of faith does best together, and the questions would be focused on discussing the assets the church has to address the needs in your community that are trauma-related. Therefore, a question like "What do you see as the most significant social issue facing our surrounding community?" might be great for a **World Café** and a launching point for shaping a trauma-informed outreach, while a better **Appreciative Inquiry** question would be, "When has our church/fellowship best supported the needs in our community through the investment of our time and energy?" The difference is that the first question focuses on the needs of the larger community, while the second should illicit responses that suggest how the Spirit has already moved in your fellowship together!

Discuss:

- As you think about the materials covered over the last seven weeks, who else in your church needs to hear about ACEs, trauma, and trauma-informed ministry principles?
- What do you think about Chaplain's Chris' take on how the Spirit might speak to your group about the "next steps" in trauma-informed ministry? What questions might you ask at a "World Café" or "Appreciative Inquiry" time that would help you get the feedback from your faith community you'd need to discern where you might go next in exploring compassionate care to hurting children and individuals?

[9] http://www.theworldcafe.com/wp-content/uploads/2015/07/Cafe-To-Go-Revised.pdf

[10] https://appreciativeinquiry.champlain.edu/

Read: Luke 14:25-34 (NLT)

 25 A large crowd was following Jesus. He turned around and said to them, 26 "If you want to be my disciple, you must, by comparison, hate everyone else—your father and mother, wife and children, brothers and sisters—yes, even your own life. Otherwise, you cannot be my disciple. 27 And if you do not carry your own cross and follow me, you cannot be my disciple.

28 "But don't begin until you count the cost. For who would begin construction of a building without first calculating the cost to see if there is enough money to finish it? 29 Otherwise, you might complete only the foundation before running out of money, and then everyone would laugh at you. 30 They would say, 'There's the person who started that building and couldn't afford to finish it!'

31 "Or what king would go to war against another king without first sitting down with his counselors to discuss whether his army of 10,000 could defeat the 20,000 soldiers marching against him? 32 And if he can't, he will send a delegation to discuss terms of peace while the enemy is still far away. 33 So you cannot become my disciple without giving up everything you own.

34 "Salt is good for seasoning. But if it loses its flavor, how do you make it salty again?

Discuss:

- Why is it important to "count the cost" of discipleship? What might it cost you, or your church, to consider ministry to traumatized children or adults?

- The idea of "hating" one's own family or carrying our own cross in order to follow Jesus is a difficult one to accept. When thinking about the sacrifice required to explore discipleship in a deeper way by engaging in trauma-informed ministry, what do you think Jesus would say to encourage you?

 Applying science, applying the Word:

Please read aloud the following from Chaplain Chris…

Perhaps you recognize these questions for ministry that address the needed six key principles to a trauma-informed approach, first discussed in week 2? Take a moment to read through these again, and circle the one question you think is most important for your group to answer next. Then, after you've read them all, you'll have a chance to share why you circled the question you did (and perhaps you'll even have some time to discuss possible answers!):

1. **Safety**: Not only is physical safety important for those coming into a worshipping community, but emotional and relational safety plays an important role as well. Only when we feel safe can we begin to trust. So, ask yourselves: *Is there structure in place that allows for vulnerable people to feel included and protected within the worshipping community? How do we express to those visiting that they will be kept safe and be provided emotional and relational safety?*

2. **Trustworthiness and Transparency**: Once safe, we can learn to trust. Trustworthiness and transparency then help that trust take root and grow into authentic relationship. So, ask yourselves: *Is authenticity a characteristic valued highly within your community of faith? Do those in ministry leadership appear as broken people in need of God's grace, just as those they minister to? Are confidences kept?*

3. **Peer support**: It may be impossible to recover from traumatic experience alone, and God has called your community together to be an expression of the Body of Christ—each member having a part. Furthermore, it is too much for a church to require that pastoral leaders, clergy, or priests bear the load of supporting the entire community. Peer support is vitally important in a trauma-informed ministry. So, ask yourselves: *Does the church go beyond being friendly to being a place someone can make friendships? Can a traumatized person find a listening ear and a welcome with others that are walking the same road to recovery, grace, and love of self and others? Can this happen both in large group and small group settings? Are ministry leaders modeling self-care through their personal practices?*

4. **Collaboration and mutuality**: Knowing what you don't know can be a gift, as long as you are willing to reach out and accept the wisdom of others! Ministry is best done WITH people than FOR people, and is definitely superior than that done TO people. So, ask yourself: *Does the church view its ministry to victimized people, traumatized individuals, and vulnerable children as integral to its call to Kingdom work for God or is it simply a niche ministry? Can the church work with others, even across ideological and denominational lines, for the betterment of hurting people?*

5. **Empowerment, voice and choice**: Building upon the last principle, collaboration should include involving those that you hope to benefit by becoming trauma-informed. Each worshipping community has both written and unwritten rules about who gets to make decisions. In light of this reality, ask yourselves: *Are those that are ministered to also given opportunity and empowered to minister within the church, understanding that they bring value and wisdom to the worshipping community? Are they fully integrated into the life of the church and given a voice for self-advocacy as well as outreach and mission?*

6. **Cultural, Historical, and Gender Issues**: Just as trauma is experienced individually and each one of us responds differently, trauma can affect us in varying ways depending on other factors that define us socially. Given this dynamic nature of how trauma is experienced, consider the following questions: *Does the church recognize the unique cultural issues sometimes bound up with trauma? Within the context of what has defined your worshipping community, is there room for the expression of faith and practice in ways that honor the unique cultural, historical, and gender backgrounds of those you seek to serve?*

Parting questions:

- **What question did you circle as the most important one for your group to address first? Why did you choose the question you did?**
- **How might your group address the issues raised by the questions asked above? How do you see these principles as necessary guidelines for shaping your future trauma-informed ministry?**

Close in Prayer:

"Jesus, when you concluded your earthly ministry, you promised your disciples something—someone—greater than having your physical presence among them. You promised the Holy Spirit, and that that Spirit would lead, guide, convict, and speak to us in our need. Holy Spirit, make good on that promise! Show us where we go from here and what our next steps in ministry should be. Our desire is to take your healing power and apply it in areas of deep woundedness and hurt. We know that there is no trauma that is greater than your ability to bring healing and hope. By your grace and mercy, empower us to be your servants to carry out that ministry of healing and hope. In your name, and with your leading, we pray. Amen."

Bonus materials: Advocating for Rachel

Intermountain Board member, Crystal Amundson

Note: *Crystal Amundson LCPC, RPT-S is the founder of Relating Play and works in private practice as a child & family therapist in Billings, Montana. Crystal specializes in Play Therapy, working with children ages 2-12, alongside their caregivers. She is a previous employee and current board member at Intermountain. Her passion and expertise is in the field of early childhood mental health. Crystal prepared this case study with accompanying prompts for action by faith-based groups and community groups that hope to make a difference in the lives of children at risk in the community. I had the pleasure of editing an excellent presentation she made to the Helena Ministerial Association in the Fall of 2015, and I am sure will be a blessing to any faith community seeking to become trauma-informed! -Chris H.*

Instructions for large group use: This case study is an effective communication tool for showing large groups, whether a ministerial association, ecumenical group, or your own congregation how the community of faith can engage in issues of children's mental health and support resilience in their context. It can be especially effective if you, as the main narrator, recruit several other readers to stand up among the audience at each break in the story to read the bulleted suggestions!

The story I'd like to share with you isn't one child's story. But it is a compilation of hundreds of true stories from children that have crossed my path since I began this work. My work started in the classrooms and cottages of Intermountain's residential program in Helena, Montana. I moved to Washington for my education and worked with children in outpatient therapy, crisis shelters, and psychiatric hospitals. I started my therapist career in Denver, Colorado doing outpatient therapy, and then did school-based therapy once I moved back to Helena. I now have a private practice with a focus on therapy, training, and supervision. Every detail in the story I'm sharing is a piece of someone's journey, and I'm grateful that you've given me time to share a bit about them with you, the reader. Because **YOU** are the game changers. And my prayer is that you hear this story with ears for opportunity. **To help, I'll pause in the telling of Rachel's story to provide bulleted points where faith communities can make a real difference.**

Now, let me introduce you to Rachel. Rachel is the second of three children. When she was born her parents were married and looked pretty average to their family, friends, and faith community. This lasted until shortly after her first birthday, when Rachel's dad was laid off his job and coped with the stress by abusing drugs. He became physically violent towards Rachel's mom and her older brother. They lost their home and for nearly three years Rachel's life was filled with domestic violence, homelessness, and neglect. What could have helped Rachel and her family in her first three years of life?

- **Be aware of the warning signs of substance abuse, homelessness, and domestic violence. Everyone is at risk, regardless of income or race or employment.**

- **Post fliers and pamphlets in your community spaces, educating your congregation about warning signs.**

- **Provide space for support groups and 12 step programs to meet. Safe, consistent spaces are a blessing.**

- **Sometimes, people are aware of the abuse or homelessness, but local resources are full. Help increase resources by volunteering with local organizations like food banks, homeless shelters, and homes for those facing domestic violence.**

On Rachel's fourth birthday, her mom took her and her siblings to a restaurant to celebrate. While there, they ran into a friend of her mom's, who questioned Rachel's brother about bruising on his face and neck. He was too scared to answer, but Rachel's mom burst into tears as she described the violent attack by Rachel's dad. Overwhelmed by guilt and fear, Rachel's mom said she was going to the bathroom and left the restaurant through the back door. The servers were delivering Rachel's free dessert and singing "Happy Birthday" when a police officer showed up. What could have been done to help Rachel and her family while she was still in preschool?

- **Educate yourself on what state law and your faith tradition say about reporting child abuse.**

- **Facilitate training and education for volunteers in children's ministry programs. Professionals need people on the front lines being the eyes and ears for welfare concerns.**

- **Host a workshop for parents and children about healthy body image and personal safety.**

- **Develop child abuse reporting policies & procedures for your congregation. This makes a difficult thing easier to do and minimizes miscommunication.**

- **Promote finger printing and background checks for adults working with children.**

- **Increase awareness by participating in activities like April Child Abuse Prevention Month.**

Rachel and her siblings were placed in foster care, alongside thousands of other children. Her brother was six, she was four, and her sister was not quite two. Her parents were given a court ordered treatment plan to address their substance abuse and mental health needs. Rachel remained in foster care for two years. During this time, she had 3 different caseworkers. Each time the worker changed, phone calls went unreturned, court deadlines were delayed, and a bit more of Rachel's story was lost. How could the faith community have helped Rachel while she was brand new "in the system?"

- **Learn about challenges facing Child Protective Services and current legislation to address training and financial shortfalls.**

- **Increase your congregation's awareness and support of the Court Appointed Special Advocate (CASA) program. Often a child's CASA is the only person that remains with them throughout their foster care journey.**

While waiting for a decision to be made about her future, Rachel lived in 3 different foster homes. She was in her first foster home for 2 months before her dad showed up one night in the yard. He was clearly intoxicated or high on drugs and was threatening to kill the family for "stealing his kids." Rachel was immediately placed in a new foster home, and stayed there for 9 months before the foster family moved out of state. Her third foster home only had room for Rachel and her younger sister. Her brother was placed in a group home. How might have the church made a difference for Rachel and her siblings during these tumultuous years?

- **Set up a table in your building with information about how to become a foster parent.**

- **Promote opportunities for foster family training by offering your space to local agencies and posting fliers about local trainings. Even existing foster parents are often unaware of training available and find themselves unequipped and overwhelmed by the children in their home.**

- **Create dedicated bible studies or small groups for adults who are foster parenting or raising extended family members (kinship care). It can be a very isolating experience and safe communities are crucial.**

Through the tumult of the previous four years, Rachel and her sister moved into the third home and stayed there for a little over a year while her mom completed the requirements with social services needed to regain custody. Rachel's dad never followed through with his substance abuse treatment and a permanent order of protection was filed with the court. Rachel & her siblings moved back in with her mom on her 6th birthday, and she was relieved that the singing and cake were forgotten in the hustle of paperwork and belongings and goodbyes.

Rachel was glad to be back with her mom, but wary of her ability to parent. Over the last four years, Rachel had been the most consistent person in her baby sister's life. Now that they were back with mom, Rachel would frequently fake illness to stay out of school and be home with her sister. While Rachel's mom wanted the best for her kids, she struggled with depression. When she worked, she struggled to find safe childcare. When she quit, she felt overwhelmed by financial burdens. She isolated from others. Stopped answering the phone when the school called about her son's behavior concerns.

Her mother let Rachel take care of the cooking and cleaning. While the arrangement had its problems, it kept Rachel busy enough to avoid the anger, confusion, and fear that had built up over the last five years. Rachel could keep it all bottled up—except around her birthday. Then, the memories of mean daddy and restaurant police visits made the feelings too big to ignore.

On her 8th birthday, Rachel's teacher led the class in a round of "Happy Birthday." Rachel began to scream at the top of her lungs, begging them to stop. Confused, the well-meaning teacher stepped in to contain Rachel's flailing and screaming and got an elbow to her face for her trouble. Sent to the principal's office, Rachel refused to talk and remained silent for the next two hours. During those two hours, the staff started to talk to each other about the girl who had flown under the radar. Rachel wasn't a behavior concern. But she had no friends. She didn't make eye contact with adults. She snuck food from the garbage during lunch. No one saw this outburst coming because no one really saw

Rachel. Rachel had become skilled at hiding her pain and trauma, and an overburdened school system cooperated in Rachel's avoidance. What would have made the difference?

- **Schools are the most common place disclosures of abuse and neglect are made. Show support for schools by volunteering time with students or preparing projects for teachers. Start with the teachers in your congregation or the school in your neighborhood... you don't have to adopt the "poor" school in town, because childhood trauma is no respecter of race, class, or income level.**

- **Write letters of affirmation to staff at neighborhood schools. The courage needed to advocate for a hurting child comes from the encouragement you feel from the community around you. Be that support system for the teachers and staff at your community schools.**

- **Stay informed about voter initiatives and upcoming elections that will impact school facilities and resources. When basic needs are met, staff are more able to focus on the "under the radar" kids. Support school board members and administrators that want to join you in becoming "trauma-informed."**

Instead of calling home, the staff called in the school-based therapist. And while Rachel didn't talk the rest of the day, she did play. She sat in the therapy office, diapering and feeding and cuddling the baby dolls. The therapist didn't talk either, but she did create space for Rachel to feel just brave enough to return to school the next day. Rachel went home and told her mom about the baby dolls. Her mom listened, and agreed to get Rachel on the waiting list for therapy. That was a year ago. Three months ago, Rachel finally started therapy. It has taken so long for Rachel to start getting the type of help that will really bring healing to her deep hurts. What might have enabled Rachel to get that help sooner?

- **Locally, there are significant shortages of mental health therapists. Encourage social service careers within the members of your congregation by hosting volunteer and job shadowing opportunities with youth groups.**

- **Invite local social service professionals to deliver the message Sunday morning or consider a special series in an adult Sunday school class on adverse childhood experiences. Brainstorm together at the conclusion of those learning experiences what God might be calling your congregation to do in response to what you learn.**

- **Support existing social service professionals by focusing mission opportunities on collecting supplies (therapeutic games or movies) or sponsoring activities (like summer camp).**

Today, Rachel turns nine and still hates her birthday. But hopefully, by working hard in therapy, she'll begin to understand why. She will learn what it means to battle Post-Traumatic Stress Injury (PTSI, formerly "PTSD") and how to feel her anger and worry and sadness without being consumed by them. Her mom will work in family therapy to learn about parenting an angry, worried, and sad kid instead of a perfect, quiet, sneaky kid. The ending to Rachel's story isn't a happily ever after. But it is an opportunity. For her and for each of us.

"Bruised Reeds and Smoldering Wicks"

About the Author:

The Reverend Doctor Chris Haughee is a licensed minister of the Evangelical Covenant Church and has served as chaplain of Intermountain's residential services since 2012. Prior to serving at Intermountain, Chris had ministered in local churches settings, primarily in children's and youth ministries. Chris is an avid NFL fan, enjoys fly fishing, hiking, and singing while playing "camp guitar." An adoptive father to two, Chaplain Chris Haughee is an advocate for greater inclusion of foster and adoptive families in the life and ministry of local congregations. Chris' Doctorate of Ministry thesis project was on training Montana's ministries in trauma-informed interventions and approaches in order to help emotionally disturbed children and their families. Chris regularly writes for the Helena Independent Record and blogs on trauma-informed ministry issues at both ACEsConnection and Intermountainministry.org. A member of Helena's Elevate Montana group (www.elevatemontana.org), you can follow his ministry at www.intermountainministry.org or contact him at pastorhaughee@yahoo.com.

Made in the USA
San Bernardino, CA
22 January 2020